KU-014-604

RESEARCH HIGHLIGHTS IN SOCIAL WORK

11 — RESPONDING TO MENTAL ILLNESS

Kogan Page

Editor: Gordon Horobin
Secretary: Anne Forbes
Editorial Advisory
Committee:

Professor G. Rochford	University of Aberdeen
Ms J. Lishman	Social Worker — Royal Aberdeen Children's Hospital
Dr P. Seed	University of Aberdeen
Dr A. Robertson	University of Edinburgh
Dr P. Hambleton	Central Region Social Work Department (SSRG Scotland Chairman)
Mr S. Montgomery	Grampian Region Social Work Department
Mr M. Brown	Highland Region Social Work Department
Mr J. Tibbitt	Social Work Services Group

University of Aberdeen
Department of Social Work
King's College
Aberdeen

First published in 1985 by Kogan Page Ltd
120 Pentonville Road, London N1 9JN
© 1985 University of Aberdeen, Department of Social Work

British Library Cataloguing in Publication Data

Responding to mental illness. — (Research
highlights in social work; 11)
  1. Psychiatry
  I. Horobin, Gordon II. Series
  616.89'1   RC480

ISBN 1-85091-004-9 (hb)
ISBN 1-85091-005-7 (pb)

Printed in Great Britain by
Biddles Ltd, Guildford

£9-95

RA
710
RES

RESEARCH HIGHLIGHTS
IN SOCIAL WORK

11 — Responding to Mental Illness

LIST OF CONTENTS

Editorial   9
Gordon Horobin

Psychiatric Disorder in the Community and in Primary Care   12
Paul Williams

Social Factors, Psychological Distress and Mental Ill-Health   27
Roslyn H. Corney

The Psychogeriatric Patient and the Family   43
Chris Gilleard

The Effects of Mental Illness on the Family: Social Work   56
Practitioner's View
Ruth Smith and Gill West

Psychiatric Crises in the Community: Collaboration and the   71
1983 Mental Health Act
T. Booth, C. Melotte, D. Phillips, J. Pritlove, A Barritt and
R. Lightup

Mental Health Officers and the Scottish Acts of 1960 and   89
1984
Chris McGregor

Anxious? Worried? Upset? The Role of a Mental Health   97
Advice Centre
Jan McLaren and Arnold Bursill

Politics and Psychiatry: The Case of Italy   114
S.P.W. Brown

New Problems, New Responses: An Overview   130
Chris Heginbotham

Contributors

Gordon Horobin — Taught Sociology at Hull University before joining the MRC Medical Sociology Unit at Aberdeen where he was Assistant Director. He now holds appointments in the Departments of Social Work and Sociology at Aberdeen and is continuing to carry out research on aspects of General Practice.

Paul Williams — Was Senior Registrar at the Middlesex Hospital before joining the General Practice Research Unit of the Institute of Psychiatry of which he is Deputy Director. He is particularly interested in factors affecting psychotropic drug prescribing. He is also Honorary Consultant Psychiatrist at the Bethlem Royal and Maudsley Hospitals.

Roslyn Corney — Trained in psychology and social work. She is now a lecturer in the General Practice Research Unit at the Institute of Psychiatry and has been primarily involved in evaluating the effectiveness of social work attachments to general practice. She is co-editor with Dr. Anthony Clare of *Social Work and Primary Health Care*, Academic Press.

Chris Gilleard — Studied Psychology at Sheffield University, and completed his clinical psychology training at Leeds University in 1973. He previously worked in the Department of Clinical Psychology at Clifton Hospital, York, and at Edinburgh University where he carried out research into psychogeriatric day care, psychotropic drug use in institutions, and depression in old age. He is co-author, with Glenda Watt, of an advice book 'Coping with Aging Parents', and author of 'Living with Dementia'.

Ruth Smith — Trained at Manchester University as a psychiatric social worker in 1971. Worked in local authority mental health departments and post Seebohm departments in Essex before moving to Aberdeen in 1972. Currently working in Royal Cornhill Hospital. Particularly interested in the development of community provision for the mentally ill.

Steve Brown — Worked on a sociological study of mental handicap in Essex, before joining the Institute of Medical Sociology at

Aberdeen University in 1981 to carry out research on the development of policy on the location of social responsibility for dependent groups. He has now taken up a post at Loughborough University.

Chris Heginbotham
Has been National Director of MIND since 1982. Previously he worked in housing, both in the housing association and local authority sectors.

Gill West
Worked in generic social work departments in Liverpool and Bristol, before obtaining CQSW at Bristol University. Before moving to Aberdeen she worked in a child guidance clinic in Bristol and for the past five years has worked in the psychiatric field at the Royal Cornhill Hospital, specialising in rehabilitation with a specific interest in community care.

Tim Booth
Hon. Director, Joint Unit for Social Services Research, and Lecturer in Social Policy, Sheffield University. He is also editor of *Social Services Monographs: Research in Practice*.

David Phillips
Lecturer in Social Administration, Sheffield University.

Chris Melotte
Research and Forward Planning Officer, Kirklees Social Services Department.

Jeremy Pritlove
Specialist Social Worker (Mental Illness), Leeds Social Services Department.

Adrian Barritt
Research Officer, West Sussex Social Services Department.

Roger Lightup
Research Officer, Trafford Social Services Department.

Chris McGregor
Appointed first Social Work Officer to the Mental Welfare Commission in January 1985. Previously was Principal Social Worker at Royal Edinburgh Hospital (Psychiatric). During part of the 11 years at the hospital, co-ordinated the MHO service for the City of Edinburgh.

Jan McLaren
Worked originally in education before joining the Institute of Medical Sociology at Aberdeen University to work on a major study of mental handicap, later becoming co-director of the project. She was appointed Development Officer of the Aberdeen and North East Association for

Mental Health in 1983 to set up a counselling and information centre.

Arnold Bursill
Worked as a clinical psychologist in Aberdeen and was Senior Lecturer in Psychology at Aberdeen University. He is now Director of the Glasgow Mental Health Association, with a special interest in the LINK projects, while retaining a part time senior lectureship at Aberdeen.

Editorial

Gordon Horobin

Mental illness is a notoriously slippery concept. While the structure and functioning of the body are by now fairly well understood, things that go wrong with the 'mind' are strange and frightening to the sufferer and only scarcely less so for those who attempt to heal or care for them. Indeed, the very notion of 'healing' is problematical: symptoms appear and grow, sometimes they are alleviated (although we may not know how) and too frequently they persist over years. How we respond to mental illness depends a good deal upon how we perceive the complex inter-relationships between behaviour, reactions to that behaviour and the social and inter-personal contexts within which it occurs. There are those who, like Szasz [1], would hold that the only true mental illness is due to brain lesions, all else being problems of living, moral responsibility for which cannot be passed on to the caring professions. Others suggest that madness is a normal response to an insane world [2] or that our feelings of despair, anxiety or inadequacy result directly from deprivations inherent in the social and economic structure. Such ideological convictions will clearly determine the forms and targets of our interventions. Most of us, however, lacking the comfort of such certainties, take a more pragmatic approach, offering psychotropics, counselling, support or institutional care; singly, in combination or in sequence. The only thing we are sure about is our own uncertainty.

A range of responses is discussed in this volume. The first two chapters, by Paul Williams and Roslyn Corney, examine what is known about the incidence of mental problems, especially at the primary care level, and how general practitioners and other members of the primary care 'team' treat those patients who present to them. While mental problems are defined in the main as 'medical' problems, it is entirely reasonable, in the British context at least, that general practitioners take primary responsibility for screening, treating or referring their patients. It is also reasonable, given this model, that psychiatrists act as arbiters of what is or is not 'normal' behaviour, wilful deviance, illness treatable in general practice or major pathology requiring specialised intervention.

Unfortunately, such a 'medical' approach may inhibit the development of other valid 'social' responses. Perhaps as Heginbotham suggests, we should put psychiatry 'in its rightful place in one corner of the huge plane that we call human emotional or mental distress'. Failure to do so will keep the non-medical professions (including social work) and those ordinary members of the community who do the greater part of the work of caring, in their present subordinate positions, and thus prevent the fulfilment of our wish for a truly comprehensive mental health service.

One issue which is so often neglected in discussion of mental illness is the problems faced by the families of the sufferers. The chapters by Smith and West and Gilleard place the needs of family members in their rightful place. Community care often means, in (I think) Joyce Leeson's phrase, 'lumbering some poor bloody woman', and Gilleard notes that male carers tend to receive more help from both formal agencies and informal neighbourhood sources. Family members have needs at various stages of the sufferer's career, not only during home care but also at the transition points into and out of hospital care, as Smith and West point out. The notion of 'patienthood' tends to focus attention solely upon the sufferer so that those involved in comprehensive mental health care need to recognise that family members may be both carers and clients at the same time.

Crisis intervention is a relatively small part of the social worker's total case load but it is obviously problematical and can be worrying. The new legislation in both England and Wales and Scotland is too recent for practice to have become established. It is worth noting, though, that emergency admissions have not fallen in number as rapidly as might have been hoped and there are still problems of inter-professional relationships at both the personal and organisational levels. Nevertheless, the findings reported by Booth et al and McGregor suggest that, given adequate training for ASWs and MHOs, there are grounds for guarded optimism. I should at this point express my gratitude to Chris McGregor for responding to my request for a brief paper on the Scottish experience at impossibly short notice: both of us would have preferred more than the two weeks I allowed her!

The range of responses to mental illness is potentially enormous and one short collection of papers could not possibly do justice to it. Two vastly different forms of innovation are, however, discussed here. At one extreme is the radical political response represented here by *psichiatrica democratica*. Brown's paper attempts to set this 'movement' in its historical context and to evaluate the evidence on its effects. Not surprisingly, his conclusion is guarded: radical solutions require political 'muscle' and such experiments cannot easily be transplanted into less hospitable environments.

The other innovation reported here, by McLaren and Bursill, has less to do with mental *illness* and more with mental distress. Based partly on some evidence that the effectiveness of 'talking' therapies depends at least as much on the personal characteristics of the counsellor as on the theoretical basis of the intervention, the walk-in advice centre uses volunteers in a non-medical setting to help clients to identify, order and cope with their own emotional or inter-personal problems. In this respect the service might be seen as preventive, although it is interesting to note that a third of the clients had received psychiatric services previously. Whether this is seen as rehabilitative or preventive at the tertiary level may be largely an academic question. Evaluation of such projects is difficult and it may be that because some people use a variety of services, shopping around among the goods on offer, the cost-effectiveness of any one part of an array of services cannot ever be ascertained.

The decision to round off this collection with an 'overview' chapter by the director of MIND has absolved the editor from that difficult task. I am indeed doubly grateful to Chris Heginbotham because, not only has he argued convincingly the case for adequate funding for the new responses to mental illness, he also agreed to extend his contribution to cover some of the issues which the late Fred Martin had undertaken to address. Our readers will have heard of Fred's sudden death with great sadness and regret. I think he would have enjoyed reading this collection and contributing to it.

References

1. Szasz, T. *The Myth of Mental Illness*. Harper, New York, 1961.

2. Laing, R.D. *The Self and Others*. Tavistock, London, 1961.

Psychiatric Disorder in the Community and in Primary Care

Paul Williams

This chapter is concerned with psychiatric disorder in the community and in general practice settings, viewed primarily from an epidemiological perspective. The extent, nature, correlates and treatment of psychiatric disorder in these settings have been the subject of a great deal of research in recent years (Hankin & Oktay [1] and Wilkinson [2] provide annotated bibliographies). This paper is a selective review of this research.

PSYCHIATRIC DISORDER IN THE COMMUNITY, IN GENERAL PRACTICE AND IN THE SPECIALIST SETTING: A CONCEPTUAL FRAMEWORK

Goldberg and Huxley [3] are the latest in a series of workers to use the concepts of *levels* and *filters* to describe psychiatric disorder and its care (see Figure 1). Their model consists of five levels, and in order to move from one level to the next, it is necessary to pass through a filter. *Level 1* refers to psychiatric and emotional disorder in the community as a whole. A proportion of people with such disorder in the community will consult a general practitioner or another member of the primary care team, i.e. will 'pass through' *filter 1* and attain level 2. Filter 1 is thus the decision to consult and the act of consulting − i.e., is based on the concept of illness behaviour [4,5,6]. It is a process which is little influenced by doctors but greatly influenced by the way in which medical care is organised (see, for example, Andersen and Newman [7] and Andersen et al. [8]).

Level 2 consists of all psychiatric/emotional morbidity that presents in primary care. However, for a proportion of such individuals, the psychological nature of their complaint goes unrecognised (see p.9 *et seq.*). Thus, they do not pass *filter 2*, which is the process of identification and

FIGURE 1

Psychiatric disorder in the community, general practice and specialist settings (from Goldberg & Huxley [3])

LEVEL 1 | psychiatric morbidity in the community |

FILTER 1: the decision to consult

LEVEL 2 | total primary care morbidity |

FILTER 2: GP recognition

LEVEL 3 | conspicuous primary care morbidity |

FILTER 3: the decision to refer

LEVEL 4 | all psychiatric patients |

FILTER 4: the decision to admit

LEVEL 5 | psychiatric inpatients |

recognition of psychiatric morbidity in general practice, and so are referred to as the 'hidden psychiatric morbidity'.

Level 3 consists of the 'conspicuous psychiatric morbidity', i.e. that morbidity identified and recognised by the primary care team. Much of this will be managed directly in the primary care setting but a proportion will be referred to the specialist psychiatric services, i.e. will pass through *filter 3* and be identified at *level 4*. Of all the patients so referred, a proportion will be admitted to hospital (passage through *filter 4*) to reach *level 5*.

There are of course exceptions to this model (e.g., an acutely disturbed patient may go directly from home to hospital, referrals to specialist psychiatric services come from sources other than general practice) but nonetheless the model seems relevant to and appropriate for the bulk of the psychiatric morbidity in the community. It makes explicit two important issues. The *first* is that whether or not an individual becomes identified as a psychiatric patient has little or nothing to do with specialist psychiatric staff/services, except indirectly. Passage through filter 1 has to do with perception of and response to illness, and passage through filters 2 and 3 depends largely on what happens in the primary care consultation. It is only when level 4 is reached that the psychiatric services enter the picture at all, and even here the specialist staff are little concerned with the identification (as opposed to the diagnosis and management) of disorder [9,10].

The *second* issue made explicit by Goldberg and Huxley [3] in their descriptive model is, to use a somewhat mechanistic analogy, that the filters are 'differentially permeable'. They present figures which suggest that about 90 per cent of individuals with psychiatric/emotional disorders will consult their GP at least once during the year (although a much smaller proportion – between a quarter and a third – will be in *current* contact with a general practitioner [11]). There is evidence that, on average, general practitioners recognise only about two-thirds of the psychiatric morbidity that presents to them (similar information with regard to other members of the primary care team is not yet available), an issue that is discussed on pp.9-11. However, it is filter 3 that is the least permeable. Only 5-10 per cent of those individuals whose psychiatric/emotional problems are recognised by general practitioners are referred to the specialist psychiatric services [12]. Thus, the bulk of the psychiatric morbidity in the community is seen and managed solely in the primary care setting; that seen and managed by specialist psychiatric teams represents a small and, as will be seen below, an atypical proportion.

THE EXTENT OF PSYCHIATRIC DISORDER IN THE COMMUNITY

The extent of psychiatric disorder in the community (or indeed, in any setting) clearly depends on how disorder is defined. This is well exemplified by Dohrenwend and Dohrenwend [13] who reviewed more than 70 community studies of psychiatric morbidity and found that the rates varied between 1 per cent and 70 per cent. They investigated the sources of variation and found that the major influence was indeed variation in the definition of disorder.

There are essentially two different models for the definition of psychiatric disorder in community studies. The first is a *diagnosis-based model* – that is, is, the threshold for psychiatric disorder is that at which a psychiatrist (using a standardised method of assessment [14]) would make a diagnosis of psychiatric disorder according to some system such as the International Classification of Diseases. Using this approach, Wing et al. [15] found that the prevalence of 'definite' psychiatric disorder in a community sample in South London was 3.6 per cent, with a further 7.3 per cent of the sample being regarded as having 'probable' disorder.

It has been argued convincingly that such an approach to the definition of psychiatric morbidity is too restrictive for community and general practice settings [16,17,18]. An alternative, and probably more useful approach is the *'just clinically-significant psychiatric disorder'* approach of Goldberg and his colleagues [3,19]. Here, the threshold for psychiatric disorder is that at which psychiatric/emotional problems might be thought to account entirely or largely for a consultation with a general practitioner. Using a standardised method of assessment based on this approach, Goldberg et al. [20] found that the prevalence of psychiatric disorder in a community sample in Manchester was just over 18 per cent.

THE EXTENT AND NATURE OF CONSPICUOUS PSYCHIATRIC MORBIDITY IN GENERAL PRACTICE

In 1982, there were some 24,000 general practitioners in England and Wales, each looking after an average of about 2,100 patients [21]. A minority are in practice by themselves ('single-handed practitioners'), while the majority work in partnership with one or more other doctors. Over the past decade or so there has been an increasing trend towards the development of *health centres*, in which a number of general practitioners work, together with other health care professionals (e.g. nurses, health visitors, social workers) as members of a 'primary care team', in purpose built premises fully equipped with supporting services.

The general practitioner and the other members of the primary care team are, by virtue of being the providers of primary medical care to a defined segment of the population, well placed to monitor psychosocial disorder in the community. Often the assessment of any one patient/client is based not only on observations made at a single consultation, but also on professional contact with the patient and the patient's family which may extend back over many years.

Individual general practitioners' estimates of the extent of psychiatric disorder among the patients in their own practices vary widely. Shepherd et al. [12] reviewed a number of prevalence studies carried out by individual GPs, and found that the rates ranged from 6 per cent to 65 per cent. It is inconceivable that such variation could be due entirely (or even largely) to differences in patient populations: indeed, there is evidence that such figures tell us more about doctors than about the patients. Thus, in order to obtain a meaningful estimate of the extent of the conspicuous psychiatric morbidity in general practice, it is necessary to study a large number of general practitioners.

Shepherd and his colleagues [12] in a now classic study, investigated a 10 per cent sample of patients registered with 46 general practices in and around London, and the findings were summarised as follows [22]:

> 'Of some 15,000 patients at risk during a 12-month period, approximately 14 per cent consulted their doctor at least once for a condition diagnosed (by the GP) as entirely or largely psychiatric in nature. The bulk of these patients would be classifiable in the

International Classification of Diseases (ICD) as suffering from neurotic or personality disorders...a large proportion of this morbidity is made up of chronic conditions.

Emotional disorders were found to be associated with a high demand for medical care. Those patients identified as suffering from psychiatric illness attended more frequently and exhibited higher rates of general morbidity and more categories of illness per head than the remainder of patients consulting their doctor...no more than about one in 20 of the patients identified in the survey had been referred to any of the specialist mental health facilities despite what the family practitioners freely acknowledged to be the unsatisfactory nature of the treatment which they were able to provide.'

TABLE 1

Patient consulting rates per 1,000 at risk for psychiatric morbidity, by sex and diagnostic group (from Shepherd et al. [12])

	male	female	all
psychosis	2.7	8.6	5.9
mental subnormality	1.6	2.9	2.3
dementia	1.2	1.6	1.4
neurosis	55.7	116.6	88.5
personality disorder	7.2	4.0	5.5
FORMAL PSYCHIATRIC ILLNESS*	67.2	131.9	102.1
psychosomatic conditions	24.5	34.5	29.9
organic illness with 'psychiatric overlay'	13.1	16.6	15.0
psychosocial problems	4.6	10.0	7.5
PSYCHIATRIC ASSOCIATED CONDITIONS*	38.6	57.2	48.6
TOTAL PSYCHIATRIC MORBIDITY*	97.9	175.0	139.4
no. of patients at risk	6783	7914	14697

*These totals cannot be obtained by adding the rates for the relevant diagnostic groups, since some patients were assigned more than one diagnosis.

Table 1 shows the distribution of psychiatric diagnoses made by the general practitioners in Shepherd et al.'s study [12]. It can be seen that psychosis — serious mental illness — accounts for less than 5 per cent of the recognised morbidity: this contrasts sharply with the distribution of morbidity seen in psychiatric outpatient clinics and inpatient samples, where psychosis accounts for some 25 per cent and 70 per cent respectively [23]. More recently, studies using validated measures of psychiatric morbidity have confirmed that there is a gradient of severity of illness from community, through general practice and outpatient samples, to inpatients [15,20,24].

As mentioned above, Shepherd and his colleagues [12] found that psychiatric morbidity in general practice was often associated with physical morbidity, both major and minor. Such findings have been repeatedly confirmed since [1,25,26,27]. There is also evidence (reviewed by Jones and Vischi [28]) for a so-called 'offset' effect: that is, appropriate treatment of the psychiatric condition results in a decrease in consulting for physical morbidity.

There is also much evidence to show that psychiatric morbidity in general practice is associated with a wide variety of social disabilities and dysfunctions, the nature and management of which will be dealt with elsewhere in this volume. However, in Shepherd's study [12], social factors were thought by the GPs to be important in the aetiology of a substantial minority of the identified psychiatric disorders. Subsequent studies have shown that patients identified as 'neurotic' by their general practitioner have more social difficulties than matched controls [29,30,31]. Using a standardised interview to assess social dysfunction, such patients have been found, as compared with the controls, to have

> 'limited or conflict-ridden relationships with neighbours, relatives and work colleagues, an excess of problems with spouses and children, and a significantly less satisfactory adjustment to their life situation' [32].

THE RECOGNITION OF PSYCHIATRIC MORBIDITY IN GENERAL PRACTICE

It has earlier been indicated that general practitioners fail to recognise between one-third and one-half of the psychiatric morbidity that presents to them, so that rates for the 'true prevalence' of psychiatric disorder in general practice attenders are of the order of 25-35 per cent [33,34,35,36].

It is of interest and importance, both academically and practically, to investigate factors which lead to the under-identification of psychiatric disorder. There is evidence to suggest that both patient and doctor characteristics are relevant.

With regard to the *patient characteristics*, Goldberg and Blackwell [33] found that patients whose psychiatric morbidity remained hidden tended to present their complaints in physical rather than psychological terms. Apart from a small group of patients who presented with a new and serious physical symptom (e.g. a breast lump) and in whom the oncomitant psychological distress was missed, there was a substantial group who presented either with a trivial physical complaint or with an exacerbation of a longstanding physical problem which was itself of little consequence. However the physical nature of the symptom was taken at face value and the psychological and emotional reasons for consulting were not explored.

With regard to the *doctor characteristics*, the large between-GP variation in rates of conspicuous psychiatric disorder has already been alluded to. Such variation raises the question of differences in the ability of general practitioners to detect psychiatric disorder, and two separate apects of this ability have been identified [3]. First, a GP may have a consistent tendency to over - or under-identify psychiatric morbidity: this general tendency is referred to as *bias*. There is evidence that it is largely determined by factors such as personality, attitudes, training and experience. Quite separate from this is the ability to identify accurately psychiatric disorder in an individual patient or a series of patients. This is referred to as *accuracy*, and is influenced largely by the nature of the doctor's behaviour during the consultation. There is evidence that such behaviour can be modified by videotape feedback training, and that such training results in general practitioners improving their accuracy in identifying psychiatric disorder [37].

An important issue is whether or not the identification of psychiatric disorder in this way makes any difference to the outcome. Johnstone and Goldberg [38] identified a series of general practice patients with hidden psychiatric morbidity by means of a screening questionnaire and randomly allocated them to two groups. For the first (the treatment group) the GP was informed of the patient's psychiatric morbidity so that he could institute treatment if he so desired, while for the second group (the control group) he was not. At three months, significantly more of the treated group were symptom free. At one year follow up, there was a significant difference (treatment better than control) for the patients who had been more severely ill at the beginning of the study, but no difference for the less severely ill. There was also evidence that identification of psychiatric disorder altered consulting behaviour: patients in the treatment group increased their consultations for emotional complaints during the follow up year, but at the expense of consultations for physical complaints. While this study is important, there were, as the authors recognised, a number of limitations, so that further studies are required before the issue can be regarded as settled.

THE MANAGEMENT OF PSYCHIATRIC DISORDER IN GENERAL PRACTICE

Faced with a patient identified as suffering from a psychiatric/emotional problem, the general practitioner has available a variety of management strategies. The GP could, for example, treat the patient *him/herself*, either with drugs or with some form of 'talking treatment'. Alternatively (or additionally) *other members of the primary care team* could be involved, or the patient may be *referred for a specialist opinion* (i.e., the patient will pass through filter 3 and be identified at level 4). Brief reference will be made here to the use of psychotropic drugs in general practice, and to aspects of referral for specialist psychiatric opinion.

The Use of Psychotropic Drugs in General Practice

One of the most commonly employed treatments for psychiatric disorder in general practice is the prescription of a psychotropic drug [12]. About one-sixth of all drugs prescribed by general practitioners are for a drug classed as psychotropic: in 1977, some 45 million prescriptions for psychotropic drugs were dispensed at retail pharmacies in England. The department of health and social security's annual statistics of general practitioner prescribing (based on prescriptions dispensed at retail pharmacies) show that until the late 1970's, there were large annual increases in the number of prescriptions for non-barbiturate hypnotics, tranquillisers and antidepressants: however, since 1978, psychotropic prescribing has decreased. Similar trends have been found in the USA and in many European countries [39].

The increasing prescription of hypnotics, tranquillisers and antidepressants has given rise to much critical comment. However, there is strong evidence from population surveys (reviewed by Williams [40]) that the proportion of the population who *consume* a psychotropic did not increase during the late 1960's and early 1970's. This discrepancy between prescription and consumption can be accounted for by two factors [40]. *First*, there is evidence that *compliance has decreased*: that is, the extent to which patients disregard the advice of their doctor has increased, particularly with regard to drug consumption [41]. *Second*, there has been an *increase in the duration of treatment* with psychotropic drugs in general practice. Although the majority of patients treated with psychotropic drugs in general practice stop treatment within a few weeks, a proportion are found to be still receiving treatment months, or even years, later [42,43]. There is evidence that this proportion has increased markedly over the past ten years or so [44], a trend that gives rise to much concern in the light of recent studies on the dependence-producing properties of benzodiazepines [45].

A recent study [46] indicated that three sets of factors were related to the duration of treatment. *First*, there were two factors relating to the patient: a history of previous psychotropic drug use was related to more lengthy treatment, as was, for women only, the presence of 'social problems' (as recognised by the GP). *Second*, there was the passage of time: imagine two patients identical in every respect except that one has been treated with a tranquilliser for one month and the other for two months. All other things being equal, the second patient will be less likely to discontinue treatment, i.e. the passage of time (in this case, one month) has adversely affected the patient's chances of coming off the medication. *Third*, there were differences between general practitioners which were independent of the patient factors. Indeed, there was evidence to suggest that some of the general practitioners in the study interacted with their patients in such a way as to (presumably unintentionally) promote long term psychotropic drug use.

Referral for Specialist Psychiatric Opinion

On average, a general practitioner will refer less than ten new patients each year to the specialist psychiatric services [47].

As has already been indicated, referred patients are not a random sample of the conspicuous psychiatric morbidity. Filter 3 is 'selectively permeable' to younger people [12], men [48], the more severely ill and the psychotic [49], persons living closer to the hospital [50] and the middle class [51], although this last finding has not always been confirmed [52].

These findings, however, tell us little about a GP's motives for referring a patient. Brook [53] put forward what he considered to be the four main motives for referral. They were (i) the GP requiring an expert opinion, so that he himself can continue treatment armed with this extra knowledge; (ii) the GP wanting a specialist treatment, unavailable in general practice, to be provided; (iii) the GP wanting to share the burden of responsibility for a patient for whom little can be done, and (iv) the GP wanting temporary relief from a demanding patient. Brook observes that the first two motives are primarily for the patient and the last two primarily for the doctor.

Kaeser and Cooper [49] investigated a sample of patients referred to the outpatient clinic at the Maudsley Hospital in London. As well as obtaining information from the records, they interviewed the referring GPs and the referred patients. In the majority of cases, the GPs wanted the hospital to take over responsibility for the patient. The findings of Johnson [54] in his study of psychiatric outpatient services in Manchester were quite different. In direct contrast to the findings of Kaeser and Cooper, the Manchester GPs, in about 50 per cent of cases, wanted 'advice only – with treatment to be continued by the general practitioner'. These disparate findings point to a wide range of opinion among GPs as to what they want from the psychiatric services, and unfortunately these needs are rarely made explicit in the letter of referral [55].

Another important reason for referral emerged from the Kaeser and Cooper study [49]. They found that 'patient request for specialist referral' was often given as the main reason for referral to the psychiatric clinic, indicating that in a substantial proportion of cases it is the patient and not the doctor who determines the referral, a finding confirmed by Johnson [54]. This is also similar to the finding of Richards [56], who reviewed a series of referrals to the Maudsley Hospital and found that about one-third had been initiated by the patient himself or a relative. Likewise, Rawnsley and Loudon [57], in their South Wales study, found that 'pressure from relatives' was an important influence on referral. One of the most important implications of these findings is summarised by Kaeser and Cooper [49] in their observation that there was

> 'an absence of firmly established clinical indications (for referral).....the selection of cases for specialist care is heavily influenced by non-clinical factors.'

IMPLICATIONS FOR FUTURE DEVELOPMENT OF SERVICES

Three models for the future development of the provision of psychiatric care to the community as a whole present themselves. The *'replacement'* model is a notion whereby specialist mental health care workers replace the general practitioner as the 'primary contact' for individuals with psychiatric/emotional problems. This has until recently been the prevalent view in the USA, as witnessed by the growth of community mental health centres [58,59]. The underlying principle, however, runs contrary to the World Health Organisation policy for primary care [60], and it has been argued that it is not widely appropriate in the context of the primary care structure in Great Britain [61]. The *'increased throughput'* model suggests that while the general practice team should retain the role of first contact, referral of more patients for specialist psychiatric care should be encouraged (a position favoured, in the early 1970's, by the Royal College of Psychiatrists [62]). There is evidence to suggest, however, that such an approach may not be feasible, since a large increase in the availability of specialist facilities does not result in an increase in the referral of new patients to the specialist psychiatric services [47].

The *'liaison/attachment'* model is an approach founded on the conclusion of Shepherd et al. [12] that:

> 'administrative and medical logic alike suggest that the cardinal requirement for improvement of the mental health services in this country is not a large expansion and proliferation of psychiatric agencies, but rather a strengthening of the family doctor in his therapeutic role.'

Increasingly in Great Britain, psychiatrists and other specialist team members are going out into the community and into general practice settings, spending time advising and teaching general practitioners, and seeing patients in general practice clinics and health centres. Currently, almost one-fifth of the consultant psychiatrists in England and Wales spend on average one session per week in this way, and a wide variety of advantages for patients, general practitioners and specialist staff, have been claimed for this way of working [63].

Clearly, the most appropriate approach to the development of psychiatric care in the community will be pluralistic. However, the work reviewed here suggests that the role of general practice is crucial. As indicated by the World Health Organisation working party on Psychiatry and Primary Care [60] the essential issue is not how primary care services can fit in with specialist psychiatric services, but rather how the latter can collaborate most effectively with the former.

References

1. Hankin, J. & Oktay, J.S. *Mental Disorder and Primary Medical Care: an analytical review of the literature.* National Institute of Mental Health, Rockville, USA, 1979.

2. Wilkinson, G. *Psychiatric Disorder in Primary Care: an annotated bibliography.* National Institute of Mental Health, Rockville, USA, 1985.

3. Goldberg, D. & Huxley, P. *Mental Illness in the Community: the pathway to psychiatric care.* Tavistock Press, London, 1980.

4. Mechanic, D. 'The Concept of Illness Behaviour' *Journal of Chronic Diseases.* 15, 1962, 189-194.

5. Mechanic, D. *Medical Sociology: a selective view.* Free Press, New York, 1968.

6. Mechanic, D. *Medical Sociology.* Free Press, New York, 1978.

7. Andersen, R. & Newman, J. 'Societal and Individual Determinants of Medical Care Utilisation in the United States' *Millbank Memorial Fund Quarterly.* 51, 1973, 91-124.

8. Andersen, R., Kravits, J. & Anderson, O. *Equity in Health Services: empirical analyses in social policy.* Bellenger, Cambridge USA, 1975.

9. Scheff, T.J. *Being Mentally Ill: a sociological theory.* Weidenfeld & Nicolson, London, 1966.

10. Ingham, J. & Miller, P.M. 'The Concept of Prevalence Applied to Psychiatric Disorders and Symptoms' *Psychological Medicine.* 6, 1976, 217-225.

11. Williams, P. 'Psychological Symptoms in West London: Socio – demographic correlates and contact with health services.' Unpublished paper, Institute of Psychiatry, 1985.

12. Shepherd, M., Cooper, B., Brown, A.C. & Kalton, G. *Psychiatric Illness in General Practice.* Oxford University Press, London, 1966.

13. Dohrenwend, B.P. & Dohrenwend, B.S. 'Social and Cultural Influences on Psychopathology' *Annual Review of Psychology.* 25, 1974, 417-452.

14. Wing, J.K., Cooper, J.E. & Sartorius, N. *The Measurement and Classification of Psychiatric Symptoms.* Cambridge University Press, Cambridge, 1974.

15. Wing, J.K., Bebbington, P., Hurry, J & Tennant, C. 'The Prevalence in a General Population of Disorders Familiar to Psychiatrists in Hospital Practice'. In Wing, J.K., Bebbington, P. & Robins, L. (Eds.) *What is a Case? The problem of definition in psychiatric community surveys.* Grant MacIntyre, London, 1981, 45-61.

16. Shepherd, M. 'Beyond the Layman's Madness: the extent of psychiatric disease'. In Tanner, J.M. (Ed.) *Developments in Psychiatric Research.* Hodder & Stoughton, London, 1977, 178-198.

17. Dohrenwend, B.P., Yager, T.S., Egri, G. & Mendelsohn, F.S. 'The Psychiatric Status Schedule as a Measure of Dimensions of Psychopathology in the General Population' *Archives of General Psychiatry.* 35, 1978, 731-737.

18. Dohrenwend, B.P., Shrout, P.E., Egri, G. & Mendelsohn, F.S. 'Nonspecific Psychological Distress and Other Dimensions of Psychopathology' *Archives of General Psychiatry.* 37, 1980, 1229-1236.

19. Goldberg, D., Cooper, B., Eastwood, M.R., Kedward, H.B. & Shepherd, M. 'A Standardised Psychiatric Interview for Use in Community Surveys' *British Journal of Preventive and Social Medicine.* 24, 1970, 18-23.

20. Goldberg, D., Kay, C. & Thompson, L. 'Psychiatric Morbidity in General Practice and the Community' *Psychological Medicine.* 6, 1976, 565-569.

21. Department of Health and Social Security. *On the State of Public Health.* HMSO, London, 1982.

22. Shepherd, M. 'General Practice, Mental Illness and the British National Health Service' *American Journal of Public Health*. 64, 1974, 230-232.

23. Marks, I.M. 'Research in Neurosis: a selective review' *Psychological Medicine*. 3, 1973, 436-454.

24. Sims, A.C. & Salmon, P. 'Severity of Symptoms of Psychiatric Outpatients' *Psychological Medicine*. 5, 1975, 62-66.

25. Eastwood, M.R. & Trevelyan, M.H. 'Relationship between Physical and Psychiatric Disorder' *Psychological Medicine*. 2, 1972, 363-372.

26. Eastwood, M.R. *The Relation between Physical and Mental Illness*. University Press, Toronto, 1975.

27. Hankin, J., Steinwachs, D.M., Regier, D.A., Burns, B.J., Goldberg, I.D. & Hoeper, E.W. 'Use of General Medical Care Services by Persons with Mental Disorders' *Archives of General Psychiatry*. 39, 1982, 225-231.

28. Jones, K.R. & Vischi, T. 'Impact of Alcohol, Drug Abuse and Mental Health Treatment on Medical Care Utilisation' *Medical Care*. 17, suppl. 2, 1979, 1-82.

29. Sylph, J., Kedward, H.B. & Eastwood, M.R. 'Chronic Neurotic Patients in General Practice' *Journal of the Royal College of General Practitioners*. 17, 1969, 162-170.

30. Cooper, B. 'Clinical and Social Aspects of Chronic Neurosis' *Proceedings of the Royal Society of Medicine*. 65, 1972, 509-512.

31. Cooper, B. 'Social Correlates of Psychiatric Illness in the Community'. In McLachlan, G. (Ed.) *Approaches to Action*. Oxford University Press, London, 1972, 65-70.

32. Clare, A.W. & Cairns, V. 'Design, Development and Use of a Standardised Interview to assess Social Maladjustment and Dysfunction in Community Studies' *Psychological Medicine*. 8, 1978, 589-604.

33. Goldberg, D. & Blackwell, B. 'Psychiatric Illness in General Practice' *British Medical Journal*. ii, 1970, 439-443.

34. Hoeper, E.W., Nycz, G.R., Cleary, P.D., Regier, D.A. & Goldberg, I.D. 'Estimated Prevalence of RDC Mental Disorder in Primary Care' *International Journal of Mental Health*. 10, 1979, 6-15.

35. Marks, J., Goldberg, D. & Hillier, V.F. 'Determinants of the Ability of General Practitioners to Detect Psychiatric Illness' *Psychological Medicine*. 9, 1979, 337-353.

36. Skuse, D. & Williams, P. 'Screening for Psychiatric Disorder in General Practice' *Psychological Medicine*. 14, 1984, 365-377.

37. Goldberg, D., Steele, J., Smith, C. & Spivey, L. 'Training Family Doctors to recognise Psychiatric Illness with Increased Accuracy' *Lancet*. ii, 1980, 521-523.

38. Johnstone, A. & Goldberg, D. 'Psychiatric Screening in General Practice' *Lancet*. i, 1976, 605-608.

39. Marks, J. 'The Benzodiazepines: an international perspective' *Journal of Psychoactive Drugs*. 15, 1983, 137-149.

40. Williams, P. 'Patterns of Psychotropic Drug Use' *Social Science and Medicine*. 17, 1983, 645-851.

41. Cartwright, A. 'Prescribing and the Doctor/Patient Relationship'. In Hasler, J. & Pendelton, D. (Eds.) *Essays on Doctor-Patient Communication*. Academic Press, London, 1984, 177-192.

42. Parish, P. 'The Prescribing of Psychotropic Drugs in General Practice' *Journal of the Royal College of General Practitioners*. 21, suppl. 1, 1971, 1-77.

43. Williams, P., Murray, J. & Clare, A.W. 'A Longitudinal Study of Psychotropic Drug Prescription' *Psychological Medicine*. 12, 1982, 201-206.

44. Marks, J. 'Benzodiazepines – for good or for evil?' *International Pharmacopsychiatry*. In print.

45. Owen, R.T. & Tyrer, P. 'Benzodiazepine Dependence: a review of the evidence' *Drugs*. 25, 1983, 385-398.

46. Williams, P. 'Factors Influencing the Duration of Treatment with Psychotropic Drugs in General Practice' *Psychological Medicine*. 13, 1983, 623-634.

47. Williams, P. & Clare, A.W. 'Changing Patterns of Psychiatric Care' *British Medical Journal*. i, 1981, 375-377.

48. Hopkins, P. & Cooper, B. 'Psychiatric Referral from a General Practice' *British Journal of Psychiatry*. 115, 1969, 1163-1174.

49. Kaeser, A. & Cooper, B. 'The Psychiatric Patient, the General Practitioner and the Outpatient Clinic' *Psychological Medicine*. 1971, 312-325.

50. Robertson, N.C. 'Variations in Referral Patterns to the Psychiatric Services by General Practitioners' *Psychological Medicine*. 9, 1979, 355-364.

51. Brown, G.W. & Harris, T. *The Social Origins of Depression*. Tavistock, London, 1978.

52. Hurry, J., Tennant, C. & Bebbington, P. 'The Selective Factors leading to Psychiatric referral' *Acta Psychiatrica Scandinavica*. Suppl. 285, 1980, 314-323.

53. Brook, A. 'An Aspect of Community Mental Health: consultative work with general practice teams' *Health Trends*. 10, 1978, 37-39.

54. Johnson, D.A.W. 'A Further Study of Psychiatric Outpatient Services in Manchester' *British Journal of Psychiatry*. 122, 1973, 301-306.

55. Williams, P. & Wallace, B.B. 'General Practitioners and Psychiatrists – Do They Communicate?' *British Medical Journal*. i, 1974, 505-507.

56. Richards, H. 'Some Factors Determining the Referral of Outpatients to a Psychiatric Hospital by General Practitioners'. M. Phil. dissertation, University of London, 1960.

57. Rawnsley, K. & Loudon, J.B. 'Factors Influencing the referral of Patients to Psychiatrists by General Practitioners' *British Journal of Preventive and Social Medicine*. 16, 1962, 174-182.

58. Fink, P.J. & Oken, D. 'The Role of Psychiatry as a Primary Care Speciality' *Archives of General Psychiatry*. 33, 1976, 998-1003.

59. Jones, K. 'Integration or Disintegration in the Mental Health Services' *Journal of the Royal Society of Medicine*. 72, 1979, 640-648.

60. World Health Organisation. 'Psychiatry and Primary Medical Care'. W.H.O. Regional Office for Europe, Copenhagen, 1973.

61. Clare, A.W. 'Community Mental Health Centres' *Journal of the Royal Society of Medicine*. 73, 1980, 75-79.

62. Williams, P. & Clare, A.W. *Psychosocial Disorders in General Practice*. Academic Press, London, 1979.

63. Strathdee, G.M. & Williams, P. 'A Survey of Psychiatrists in Primary Care: the silent growth of a new service' *Journal of the Royal College of General Practitioners*. 34, 1984, 615-618.

Social Factors, Psychological Distress and Mental Ill-Health

Roslyn H. Corney

INTRODUCTION

While there are individual and biological differences in the extent to which people are vulnerable to psychological symptoms and mental illness, the evidence of many studies suggests that social factors are also of fundamental importance. However, social factors not only influence whether a person develops symptoms of psychological distress, but they also determine what types of symptoms are exhibited and what the person does about them. This will include what illness behaviours individuals will execute; for example, whether they visit their family doctor or confide in a close friend, or start to drink more heavily. In addition, social factors have an effect on whether the doctor involved will recognise the symptoms as an illness and what treatment he decides to give.

Many things other than the occurrence of symptoms of psychological distress have to happen before an individual is recognised by a doctor or by others as having a psychiatric illness. While Goldberg & Huxley [1] suggest a series of filters through which potential psychiatric patients have to pass (see Chapter 1), Cochrane [2] describes a more detailed model elaborating further on the cognitive processes occurring in the potential patient. Social factors have their effect on each stage of this process.

The situation is made even more complex by the fact that a change in social factors often results from a person developing a psychiatric illness such as schizophrenia or depression and that social factors also affect duration of illness and relapse rates. Thus it is often difficult to ascertain whether the social factor, such as a marital problem, results from the illness or is a precipitant to it.

The literature assessing the role of social factors in psychiatric disorder may be broadly classified into that concerned with chronic social difficulties, life events, social supports and demographic variables such as sex, employment and marital status.

CHRONIC SOCIAL DIFFICULTIES

Chronic social difficulties such as financial hardship, social isolation, migration and low social class have been shown to be associated with increased prevalence of mental illness. Many of the classic studies have found that first admissions for schizophrenia are more prevalent in the poor, socially disorganised central areas of cities [3,4] and debate has centred around the question of whether the high rates of schizophrenia in certain impoverished neighbourhoods were due to schizophrenics drifting into the poorer,more socially disorganised areas as a result of their illness (the social drift hypothesis) or whether their illness was in fact precipitated by the adverse conditions encountered in such a neighbourhood (the social stress hypothesis). The findings of Goldberg and Morrison [5] and Hare and colleagues [6] support the drift hypothesis; however, the relationship of chronic social difficulties to other illnesses, such as manic depressive psychosis or minor psychiatric morbidity, is much less clear.

In 1969, the Dohrenwends reviewed 44 studies which had attempted to test the true prevalence of psychiatric disorder in community populations and found that the most consistent result was an inverse relationship between social class and reported rate of psychological disorders [7]. They analysed the results of these studies in order to find out whether this relationship could primarily be explained as evidence of social causation, with the environmental pressures associated with low social status causing the social pathology, or alternatively as evidence of social selection with pre-existing psychological disorder leading to a decline in social status. Their results were not clear and they concluded that the association was in fact due to a combination of these effects. They considered that psychological symptoms in community populations were of two main types; those generated by social situations and those mainly generated by personality defects, probably genetic in origin.

LIFE EVENTS

More recently, research has been directed towards a class of stressful situations or life events which occur in the natural course of everyday life, such as marriage, bereavement, moving house and childbirth. These events may be stressful to some individuals but not to others.

A higher frequency of such events has been found in schizophrenics prior to their illness [8,9] and in depressed outpatients [10,11,12] than in the general population. Epidemiological studies have also shown that life events are associated with untreated symptoms in the community [12,13,14] and with the onset of depression in general practice patients [15].

Brown and his colleagues [8] have attempted to record life events in a systematic fashion, measuring their severity, their exact timing, their objective severity and whether they could have possibly been influenced by the patient. This detailed information is necessary so that the increased number of life events reported by ill subjects could not be attributed to the psychological symptoms bringing about the event or the symptoms disturbing the patient's recall of the severity of the event.

Brown and his colleagues in another paper [16] proposed the now generally accepted view of schizophrenic patients that 'a person predisposed for ... genetic, constitutional or other reasons ... will also have some chance of developing the disorder following life events'. Life events thus act as precipitating factors in the development of schizophrenia. However, Brown also suggests that in depressive illnesses, the condition may actually be caused by a life event rather than just precipitated. However, these findings and conclusions have been criticised by other workers in this field who point to the many methodological problems encountered and suggest that a causal connection between life events and depression should at the present time remain unspecified [17].

Brown and Harris [18] in one recent study in London attempted to connect the findings on the effects of social class and life events on the incidence of mental illness. In this study, the researchers interviewed a random sample of women living in South London and found a large social class difference in the prevalence of depression. Although the working class women had more long term social difficulties and life events which were shown to play an aetiological role, this only explained a small part of the social class difference. The workers argued that the difference was due not only to the frequency of life events and difficulties in the lower social classes but also due to the fact that the working class women were more likely to break down once these have occurred. This greater vulnerability was shown to relate to four specified social factors; the existence of an intimate confiding relationship with a husband, the number of children under the age of 14 living at home, the loss of the mother before the age of 11 and whether or not the woman was employed before the onset of illness. However, even the findings of this study have been cast in doubt. A re-analysis of Brown and Harris's data, using log-linear models, by Tennant and Bebbington [19], does not confirm this contention.

Other studies have suggested that a close relationship with a spouse or a sexual partner exercises a protective function [20,21,22], but these suggest that other social relationships may also be important, if only to a lesser extent.

SOCIAL SUPPORTS

Evidence that there is a connection between inadequate social supports and psychiatric illness has been obtained by a variety of studies. Henderson and colleagues [21] found that psychiatric patients had smaller social networks and less effective interaction with the primary attachment figure than matched controls. In another study by Henderson and colleagues [22], the researchers found that the availability and adequacy of loving, intimate relationships negatively related to the presence of neurosis. People who commit suicide and old people in the community who are mentally ill are also more likely to have had fewer social contacts [23,24,25]. These findings lend support to those of Brown and Harris [18] who suggest that lack of an intimate confiding relationship with husband or boyfriend is an important vulnerability factor increasing the effects of severe life events on women.

Social supports have also been found to reduce the psychological distress following job loss and bereavement [26,27,28], and to reduce the number of psychiatric casualties in combat situations [29].

It has been proposed that while lack of social networks is harmful, good social supports can be beneficial. The effects of social support on normal growth, different diseases, mortality and mental illness have been the subject of many reviews [30,31].

The nature of the interaction between social support and stress is still unresolved, although two major alternatives have been identified [32,33]. First, stress and social supports have their different effects on illness but each acts independently of the other [19,20]. Alternatively social support may act by decreasing the likelihood of encountering stressful life events [13], or by decreasing their impact [19].

The situation is made much more complicated by the fact that these two major alternatives may not be mutually exclusive and that life events may elicit more social support from others. As with life events, research on social supports has encountered many methodological problems with a number of confounding variables. Many of the results found by these studies could be due to neurotic symptoms leading to deficiencies in social bonds rather than vice versa; alternatively, the findings could be due to subjects, particularly the depressed, giving inaccurate and pessimistic accounts of their social situation. Individuals considered to be neurotic may also have a greater need for social relationships and hence complain when these higher expectations are not met.

OTHER SOCIAL FACTORS DETERMINING THOSE AT HIGH RISK

(a) Gender

More women than men suffer from forms of depression including minor psychiatric morbidity [34] and manic depressive psychoses [35]. They are also more likely to attempt suicide [36]. However, men have a higher risk of completed suicide [36] and of problem drinking [32,37]. There is, however, no sex difference in the prevalence of schizophrenia or senile dementia when allowance is made for the lifespan of women.

While there is a substantial female preponderance among those identified by general practitioners as psychiatrically ill (female:male ratio 1.78:1.36) a smaller proportion of these female general practice patients are referred to psychiatrists than male patients and therefore are less likely to be admitted into hospital as inpatients. The small female excess among inpatients is therefore a reflection of a very much larger female excess in the community.

The differences in vulnerability between the sexes for affective disorders may be due to biological or environmental reasons or both. Some of the differences in prevalence rates may be due to better detection and reporting of illness among women. Women are more likely to recognise psychiatric problems in themselves than are men [38], women are more likely to consult doctors [36] and doctors are more likely to detect psychiatric illness in women than in men [37]. However, even with better detecting and reporting among women, women still have higher rates [40,41] and various community samples indicate that female rates are almost double the male [1].

Are these differences biological? Are women innately more emotional than men and more prone to emotional upsets? The occurrence of premenstrual tension, post partum depression and the menopause lends support to this view, but Weissman and Klerman [40] in their review concluded that while some portion of the sex difference in depression may be explained endocrinologically, these factors are not sufficient to account for the large sex differences.

Alternatively, are women more environmentally predisposed to depression than men? Do women experience more life events, more chronic social stress or less social support than do men? Or do women report more symptoms because it is culturally more acceptable for them to do so? Are the roles of women, particularly married women, more frustrating than men's, leading to more stress and less social support?

However, comparative studies between men and women have been few, so the evidence is far from complete.

(b) Marital Status

Higher prevalence rates of illness among the separated and the divorced have been found by many studies [1,22]. This may be due to depressed or anxious individuals being more prone to marital disharmony or due to marital disharmony and lack of a supportive intimate relationship increasing an individual's vulnerability to the effects of life events. However, marital status also influences illness behaviour, with the single, separated and divorced with psychological distress more likely than the married and cohabiting to consult their general practitioners [1]. These data support the work described earlier on social networks and social support.

Economic hardship and social isolation are more common in the unmarried population and parenthood places a particular strain on the unmarried [42]. However, it may also be true that the unmarried are particularly vulnerable because of their lack of social support [43,44].

While marriage does offer a considerable degree of protection for men and women against being admitted into hospital, this is much more apparent for men than for women. Gove and his colleagues have suggested that marriage is relatively less satisfying for women than for men, with the role of housewife being inevitably unstructured, invisible and of low status [45]. However, community studies do not necessarily confirm the findings of hospital admissions and many investigations have found no relationship between marital status and psychological symptom levels in the community [46]. It is possible that paid employment may be the crucial factor in reducing the number of symptoms and the major difference between married women and married men is the probability of being in employment [2].

(c) Employment Status

Community surveys in the United States [45,46] and in the United Kingdom [47] find a higher proportion of unemployed among the depressed population than among the normals. Brown and Harris [18] also found that unemployment was one of the four specific vulnerability factors in women. Particular groups are the long term unemployed and the never employed school leavers.

In addition to the above, other factors such as migration, nationality, culture, and religious beliefs are also of crucial importance in determining community levels of morbidity as well as affecting help seeking and illness behaviour.

The study of cultural influences in Great Britain is confounded by migration. Most of the major subcultures were brought here by immigrants and thus the adults had to cope with the experiences of migration as well as those of belonging to a cultural minority. Other factors such as degree of prejudice from the host culture, degree of integration and the immigrants' socio-economic position in society are also of major importance. These factors are covered in detail elsewhere in a number of publications [2,46,48].

SOCIAL PROBLEMS ASSOCIATED WITH ILLNESS

Although there are considerable problems involved when attempting to determine the importance of social factors in the aetiology of psychological disorders, there is less difficulty in showing that changes in social factors are commonly associated with these illnesses. A higher degree of social impairment has been found in depressed patients than in normal patients [18,36,49,50] and chronic neurotics in general practice have been shown to have a greater degree of social impairment than a matched group of normal patients [51,52]. Some of these problems may occur before the illness or disorder, but the symptoms themselves, being likely to put extra strain on personal relationships as well as to affect work performance, etc., may lead to marital disharmony eventually leading to divorce and family break-up or to job loss and subsequent unemployment.

The study by Weissman and Paykel [50] compared 40 depressed female outpatients with 40 matched controls. They found highly significant differences in social role functioning between the two groups of women over all their social roles. On nearly all the items, the average rating for the normals was at the 'less impaired' end of the scales. In contrast, the depressed sample nearly always showed moderate impairment. Impairment was particularly marked for work roles, especially that of the housewife and for the intimate relationships of marriage and parenthood. The depressed patients' marital relationships were characterised by friction, poor communication, decreased affection and diminished sexual satisfaction. Friction also occurred in their relationships with their children.

Another study of general practice patients yielded similar results [51]. Neurotic patients had limited or conflict-ridden relationships with neighbours, relatives and workmates, an excess of problems with spouse and children and, overall, a less satisfactory adjustment to their life situation than a matched group of normal patients.

THE EFFECT OF SOCIAL FACTORS ON PROGNOSIS

Social factors have also been shown to play a part in the prognosis of illness, chronicity being associated with long term social difficulties. Generally, the prognosis for the acute depressive episode is good. Beck reviewed a number of studies from the era prior to antidepressants and concluded that complete symptomatic recovery occurred in 70-95 per cent of cases, although a large proportion of these cases will have a recurrence of depression at some time [53].

The prognosis for more chronic cases is much less satisfactory. Longitudinal studies in general practice suggest that those individuals who have had symptoms for more than a year tend to have illnesses continuing for many years [54,55,56]. The findings suggest the possibility of distinguishing between two broad groups of patients: short term illnesses of favourable prognosis and chronic disorder with a poor outcome [55,56,57,58].

Kedward [55] in his study found that those who had chronic social problems were more likely to become chronically neurotic and not to have improved after three years than patients without chronic problems.

Situational factors noted in these chronic patients were: severe marital disharmony, chronic housing problems, long term illness, and bereavement. Kedward concluded that a great deal of suffering could perhaps have been alleviated by social measures, altering the patient's social situation and through this his/her mental condition.

Another study of 50 non-psychotic outpatients has indicated that the patient's social circumstances affect prognosis [59,60]. The results showed that the strongest single predictor of outcome at six months was social dysfunction in the area of the patient's material and objective circumstances. Those who did not recover during this six month time period were more likely to have poor social conditions such as poor housing, inadequate financial resources and inadequate facilities for their children. Another study of general practice attenders obtained similar results [61].

The few studies that relate to prognosis rather than aetiology also demonstrate that social support plays a key role in the outcome in schizophrenia [62], depression [63] and minor psychiatric morbidity [60,61,64].

It has been found that schizophrenic patients are more likely to break down and be readmitted to hospital when they are discharged to a home with high emotional involvement (strongly expressed emotion, hostility or dominating behaviour shown towards the patient by one or more members of his family) than to a home of low emotional involvement [62,65]. Unmarried male schizophrenics were found to be particularly at risk. Schizophrenics who were discharged to homes of high emotional involvement were more likely to keep well if they became socially withdrawn, avoided their families or limited the number of hours with them.

Lack of employment is another variable which has shown to have an effect on relapse rates. The importance of employment in the successful discharge of short and long stay patients, particularly schizophrenics, has been shown by a number of researchers in this field [66,67,68].

MENTAL ILLNESS OR PROBLEMS OF LIVING?

While the terms 'disorder' and 'problem' have been frequently used in association with anxiety or depression, these states are not always abnormal and do not always constitute disorder. It is normal to feel anxious about events or activities such as changing a job or moving house. It is also normal to feel miserable after failing an examination or to grieve following the death of a close friend or relative. Intense depression may be considered to be a normal reaction to the death of one's child or spouse and lack of emotional response to such an event may be considered abnormal.

Symptoms of psychological disorder and distress range in severity forming a continuum from slight to severe; thus when can someone be considered to be reacting normally and be regarded to be suffering from a 'problem of living' and when can someone be considered to be 'ill'? The situation has been made more complicated in recent years by the fact that people are more likely to turn to medicine, particularly their family doctor, with a range of problems that would not have previously been regarded as medical matters [69,70], and there is a certain amount of evidence that this trend towards seeking advice from doctors is growing [71].

This trend is probably due to a number of reasons: the greater acceptability of health problems rather than emotional or personal ones; the free availability and accessibility of doctors; the relative lack of help from community and kin-groups, especially with increased mobility; the secularisation of society; and the availability of psychotropic drugs. In effect, the tendency is to look for medical answers to social and personal problems and to medicalise life, thus giving medical labels for personal problems.

However, the situation is made even more complicated by the fact that the minor disorders such as depression and anxiety, precipitated by social stresses, are identical in symptom content with these same disorders apparently not associated with social stress.

Lewis [72] took the view that social adaptation cannot be a criterion of mental illness because criteria of social malfunction vary from population to population. He suggested that we needed to search for firmer criteria of mental illness which apply to all populations and he took the view that mental illness may be defined as qualitatively altered functions of some part of the total, such as thinking, perception or mood. Some authors assert that such firm criteria do not exist [73]. Both views accept that social deviance is not mental illness. However, as Lewis argues, to deny a social content in the idea of health is by no means denying it a social context. He concluded that 'although the social effects of disease, like the social causes, are extremely important, it is impossible to decide from them whether a condition is healthy or morbid' [72].

Resolution of this question of whether somebody can be considered mentally ill is crucial in deciding whom to treat. Those who assert that minor psychiatric morbidity is not an illness but a social reaction to factors such as poverty, poor housing or unemployment, may continue to say that doctors should not treat afflicted individuals. Treating the depressed and unhappy with psychotropic drugs, for example, can have political consequences as it reduces people's motivations to seek to change their social conditions [74]. However, leaving the individual untreated may have unfavourable consequences not only for the individual concerned, but also for others in terms of disturbed family relationships, increased sickness absence, increased impaired productivity, accidents and social problems.

IMPLICATIONS FOR THE PRACTITIONER

Increasing Levels of Social Support

While the helping professions cannot always reduce the number of life events or crises in a vulnerable individual's life, they may try to offset the damaging effects of these by increasing the social support that the individual receives from others. This may be attempted by working within the marital or family relationships or by increasing the individual's social contacts. Self help groups or groups run by a professional may often help by bringing together individuals with similar problems who can support and confide in one another [75].

However, encouraging closer relationships with the family may not always have a positive outcome. The work by Vaughn and Leff [62] has immediate relevance to those responsible for the discharge of schizophrenic patients into the community. For those with families exhibiting 'high expressed emotion', a hostel placement may be preferable to discharging the patient back home. Alternatively, steps may be taken to limit the number of hours the patient spends in close contact with his family by arranging a day hospital or work placement.

Employment and the Alleviation of Practical Problems

Another important area in which the helping professions may be of help is to encourage and assist the individual to seek and secure employment of some kind. Paid employment seems to be an important factor both in preventing relapse for those with major illnesses [66] and in the protection of women who are vulnerable to depressive disorders [18].

The findings of two clinical trials of social work carried out on general practice attenders suggested that practical help and assistance were of great importance in bringing about clinical and social improvement. The first of these studies included patients of all ages with chronic neuroses [76], and in the second study women with acute or acute and chronic depression were investigated

[77]. Practical help included the provision of information, advocacy and the direct provision of materials and services.

In the latter study of depressed women, social work involvement was found to have the most effect on patients with major marital difficulties and poor social contacts who oten had no one to confide in [77]. These results suggest that the involvement of an outsider may be of particular help to these patients who lack support from elsewhere.

Effects of Distress on the Family and Family Life

The effects of psychological disorder and distress are likely to place extra strains on relationships within the family and on outsiders, as well as the individual's work performance and management of his or her affairs. Support needs not only to be given to the suffering individual but also to the family members in order to reduce any resulting disharmony. Help also needs to be given to the sufferer so that job loss, financial problems and other difficulties are avoided if at all possible.

Acknowledgements

I would like to thank Dr. Rachel Jenkins, Consultant Psychiatrist at St. Bartholomews Hospital, for her help in the preparation of this paper.

References

1. Goldberg, D. & Huxley, P. *Mental Illness in the Community. The Pathway to Psychiatric Care.* Tavistock Publications, London, 1980.

2. Cochrane, R. *The Social Creation of Mental Illness.* Longman, London, 1983.

3. Faris, R.E.L. & Dunham, H.W. *Mental Disorders in Urban Areas: An ecological study of schizophrenia and other psychoses.* University of Chicago Press, Chicago, 1939.

4. Hare, E.H. 'Mental Illness and Social Conditions in Bristol' *Journal of Mental Science.* 102, 1956, 349-357.

5. Goldberg, E.M. & Morrison, S.L. 'Schizophrenia and Social Class' *British Journal of Psychiatry.* 109, 1963, 785-802.

6. Hare, E.H., Price, J.S. & Slater, E. 'Parental Social Class in Psychiatric Patients' *British Journal of Psychiatry.* 121, 1972, 515-524.

7. Dohrenwend, B.S. *Social Status and Psychological Disorder: A Causal Inquiry*. John Wiley & Sons, London, 1969.

8. Brown, G.W., Sklair, F., Harris, T. & Birley, J.L.T. 'Life Events and Psychiatric Disorders. Part 1: Some methodological Issues' *Psychological Medicine*. 3, 1973, 74-87.

9. Paykel, E.S. 'Recent Life Events and Clinical Depression'. In Gunderson, E.K.E. & Rahe, R.H. (Eds.) *Life Stress and Illness*. Charles C. Thomas, Springfield, Illinois, 1974, 134-163.

10. Holmes, T.R. & Rahe, R.H. 'The Social Readjustment Rating Scale' *Journal of Psychosomatic Research*. 11, 1967, 213-218.

11. Paykel, E.S., Myers, J.K., Dienelt, M.N., Klerman, G.L., Lindenthal, J.J. & Pepper, M.P. 'Life Events and Depression: a controlled study' *Archives of General Psychiatry*. 21, 1969, 753 – 760.

12. Brown, G.W., Bhrolchain, M. & Harris, T.P. 'Social Class and Psychiatric Disturbance among Women in an Urban Population' *Sociology*. 9, 1975, 225-254.

13. Myers, J.K., Lindenthal, J.J. & Pepper, M.P. 'Life Events and Psychiatric Impairment' *Journal of Nervous and Mental Disease*. 152, 1971, 149-157.

14. Uhlenhuth, E.H., Lipman, R.S., Balter, M.B. & Stern, M. 'Symptoms Intensity and Life Stress in a City' *Archives of General Psychiatry*. 31, 1974, 759-764.

15. Cooper, B. & Sylph, J. 'Life Events and the Onset of Neurotic Illness: an investigation in general practice' *Psychological Medicine*. 3, 1973, 421-435.

16. Brown, G.W., Harris, T.O. & Peto, J. 'Life Events and Psychiatric Disorders. Part 2: Nature of causal link' *Psychological Medicine*. 3, 1973b, 159-176.

17. Tennant, C., Bebbington, P. & Hurry, J. 'The Role of Life Events in Depressive Illness: is there a substantial causal relation?' *Psychological Medicine*. 11, 1981, 379-389.

18. Brown, G.W. & Harris, T. *Social Origins of Depression: a study of psychiatric disorder in women*. Tavistock, London, 1978.

19. Tennant, C. & Bebbington, P. 'The Social Causation of Depression: a critique of the work of Brown and his colleagues' *Psychological Medicine*. 8, 1978, 565-575.

20. Miller, P.McC. & Ingham, J.G. 'Friends, Confidantes and Symptoms' *Social Psychiatry*. 11, 1976, 51-58.

21. Hesbacher, P.T., Rickels, K. & Goldberg, D. 'Social Factors and Neurotic Symptoms in Family Practice' *American Journal of Public Health*. 65, 1975, 148-155.

22. Henderson, S., Byrne, D.G., Duncan-Jones, P., Scott, R. & Adcock, S. 'Social Relationships, Adversity and Neurosis: a study of associations in a general population sample' *British Journal of Psychiatry*. 136, 1980, 574-583.

23. Nielsen, J. 'Geronto-Psychiatric Period Prevalence Investigation in a Geographically Delineated Population' *Acta Psychiatrica Scandinavica*. 38, 1962, 307-310.

24. Kay, K.D.W., Beamish, P. & Roth, M. 'Old Age Mental Disorders in Newcastle-upon-Tyne. Part II: a study of possible social and medical causes' *British Journal of Psychiatry*. 110, 1964, 668-682.

25. Sainsbury, P. 'Suicide: Opinions and Facts' *Proceedings of the Royal Society of Medicine*. 66, 1973, 579-587.

40

26. Burch, J. 'Recent Bereavement in Relation to Suicide' *Journal of Psychosomatic Research*. 16, 1972, 361-366.

27. Parkes, C.M. *Bereavement. Studies of Grief in Adult Life*. Tavistock, London, 1972.

28. Gore, S. 'The Influence of Social Support and Related Variables in Ameliorating the Consequences of Job Loss'. Unpublished doctoral dissertation, University of Pennsylvania, 1973.

29. Rose, A.M. 'Factors in Mental Breakdown in Combat'. In Rose, A.M. (Ed.) *Mental Health and Mental Disorder – a Sociological Approach*. Routledge & Kegan Paul, London, 1966.

30. Cobb, S. 'Social Support as a Moderator of Life Stress' *Psychosomatic Medicine*. 38, 1976, 5, 300-314.

31. Gore, S. 'The Influence of Social Support and Related Variables in Ameliorating the Consequences of Job Loss'. Unpublished doctoral dissertation, University of Pennsylvania.

32. Cassel, J. 'An Epidemiological Perspective of Psychosocial Factors in Disease Aetiology' *American Journal of Public Health*. 64, 1974, 11, 1040-1043.

33. Henderson, A.S. 'The Social Network, Support and Neurosis. The Function of Attachment in Adult Life' *British Journal of Psychiatry*. 131, 1977, 185-191.

34. Shepherd, M., Cooper, B., Brown, A.C. & Kalton, G.W. *Psychiatric Illness in General Practice*. Oxford University Press, London, 1966.

35. Slater, E. & Cowie, V. *The Genetics of Mental Disorder*. Oxford University Press, London, 1971.

36. Kennedy, P., Krietman, N. & Ovenstone, I.M.K. 'The Prevalence of Suicide and "Parasuicide" (attempted Suicide) in Edinburgh' *British Journal of Psychiatry*. 124, 1974, 36-41.

37. Edwards, G., Hawker, A., Hensman, C., Peto, J. & Williamson, V. 'Alcoholics Known and Unknown to Agencies: epidemiological studies in a London Suburb' *British Journal of Psychiatry*. 123, 1973, 169-183.

38. Horowitz, A. 'The Pathways into Psychiatric Treatment: some differences between men and women' *Journal of Health and Social Behaviour*. 18, 1977, 169-178.

39. Marks, J., Goldberg, D.P. & Hillier, V.F. 'Determinants of the Ability of General Practitioners to Detect Psychiatric Illness' *Psychological Medicine*. 9, 1979, 337-353.

40. Weissman, M.M. & Klerman, G.L. 'Sex Differences and the Epidemiology of Depression' *Archives of General Psychiatry*. 34, 1977, 98-111.

41. Briscoe, M.E. 'Sex Differences in Psychological Well-being' *Psychological Medicine*. 1982, Monograph Supplement 1, Cambridge University Press.

42. Pearlin, L.I. & Johnson, J.S. 'Marital Status, Life Status and Depression' *American Sociological Review*. 42, 1977, 704-715.

43. Gove, W.R. & Tudor, J.F. 'Adult Sex Roles and Mental Illness' *American Journal of Sociology*. 78, 1973, 812-835.

44. Cochrane, R. & Stopes-Roe, M. 'Women, Marriage, Employment and Mental Health' *British Journal of Psychiatry*. 139, 1981, 373 – 381.

45. Tischler, G.L., Henisz, J.E., Myers, J.K. & Boswell, P.C. 'Utilisation of Mental Health Services. Patienthood and the Prevalence of Symptomatology in the Community' *Archives of General Psychiatry*. 32, 1975a, 411-415.

46. Weissman, M.M. & Myers, J.K. 'Rates and Risks of Depressive Disorders in a U.S. Suburban Community' *Acta Psychiatrica Scandinavica*. 57, 1978, 219-231.

47. Williams, P., Jenkins, R. & Tarnopolsky, A. 'Psychotropic Drug Consumption in Unemployed Males' (in preparation).

48. Rack, P. *Race, Culture and Mental Disorder*. Tavistock, London, 1982.

49. Weissman, M.M., Paykel, E.S., Seigel, R. & Klerman, G.L. 'The Social Role Performance of Depressed Women: a comparison with a normal sample' *American Journal of Orthopsychiatry*. 41, 1971, 390-405.

50. Weissman, M.M. & Paykel, E.S. *The Depressed Woman: a Study of Social Relationships*. University of Chicago Press, Chicago, 1974.

51. Sylph, J.A., Kedward, H.B. & Eastwood, M.R. 'Chronic Neurotic Patients in General Practice. A Pilot Study' *Journal of the Royal College of General Practitioners*. 17, 1969, 162-170.

52. Cooper, B. 'Clinical and Social Aspects of Chronic Neurosis' *Proceedings of the Royal Society of Medicine*. 65, 1972, 509-512.

53. Beck, A.T. *Depression: Clinical, Experimental and Theoretical Aspects*. Harper and Row, New York, 1967.

54. Kedward, H.B. & Cooper, B. 'Neurotic Disorders in Urban Practice: a three-year follow up' *Journal of the Royal College of General Practitioners*. 12, 1966, 148-162.

55. Kedward, H.B. 'The Outcome of Neurotic Illness in the Community' *Social Psychiatry*. 4(1), 1969, 1-4.

56. Cooper, B., Fry, J. & Kalton, G.W 'A Longitudinal Study of Psychiatric Morbidity in a General Practice Population' *British Journal of Preventive and Social Medicine*. 23, 1969, 210-217.

57. Hagnell, O. *A Prospective Study of the Incidence of Mental Disorder*. Swenska Bokforlaget, Norstedts-Bonnies, Stockholm, 1966.

58. Harvey-Smith, E.A. & Cooper, B. 'Patterns of Neurotic Illness in the Community' *Journal of the Royal College of General Practitioners*. 19, 1970, 132-139.

59. Huxley, P. & Goldberg, D.P. 'Social Versus Clinical Prediction in Minor Psychiatric Disorders' *Psychological Medicine*. 5, 1975, 96-100.

60. Huxley, P.J., Goldberg, D.P., Maguire, G.P. & Kincey, V.A. 'Predictions of the Course of Minor Psychiatric Disorders' *British Journal of Psychiatry*. 135, 1979, 535-543.

61. Jenkins, R., Mann, A.H. & Belsey, M. 'Design and Use of a Short Interview to Assess Social Stress and Support in Research and Clinical Settings' *Social Science & Medicine*. 15E, 1981, 3, 195 – 203.

62. Vaughn, C.E. & Leff, J.P. 'The Influence of Family and Social Factors on the Course of Psychiatric Illness: a comparison of schizophrenic and depressed neurotic patients' *British Journal of Psychiatry*. 129, 1976, 125-127.

63. Bullock, R.C., Siegel, R., Weissman, M. & Paykel, E.S. 'The Weeping Wife: marital relations of depressed women' *Journal of Marriage and the Family*. 34, 1972, 488.

64. Holahan, C.J. & Moos, R.H. 'Social Support and Psychological Distress: a longitudinal analysis' *Journal of Abnormal Psychology*. 90, 1981, 365-370.

65. Brown, G.W., Birley, J.L.T. & Wing, S.K. 'Influence of Family Life on the Cause of Schizophrenic Disorders: a replication' *British Journal of Psychiatry*. 121, 1972, 241-258.

66. Stingham, J.A. 'Rehabilitating Chronic Neuropsychiatric Patients' *American Journal of Psychiatry*. 108, 1952, 924-928.

67. Cohen, L. 'Vocational Planning and Mental Illness' *Personnel & Guidance Journal*. 1955, 28th September.

68. Mandelbrote, B.M. & Folkland 'Some Factors Related to Outcome and Social Adjustment in Schizophrenia' *Acta Psychiatrica Scandinavica*. 27, 1961, 223-235.

69. Cartwright, A. *Patients and their Doctors*. Routledge & Kegan Paul, London, 1967.

70. Cartwright, A. & Anderson, R. *General Practice Revisited: a Second Study of Patients and their Doctors*. Tavistock, London, 1981.

71. Dunnell, K. & Cartwright, A. *Medicine Takers, Prescribers and Hoarders*. Routledge & Kegan Paul, London, 1972, 304-305.

72. Lewis, A. 'Health as a Social Concept' *British Journal of Sociology*. 4, 1953, 109-124.

73. Szasz, T.S. *The Manufacture of Madness*. Routledge & Kegan Paul, London, 1971.

74. Lader, M. 'The Social Implications of Psychotropic Drugs' *Royal Society of Health Journal*. 95(b), 1975.

75. Corney, R.H. 'Group Work with Single Parents – Participants' Impressions', Centre Eight Papers *Health and Social Service Journal*. 1978.

76. Cooper, B., Harwin, B.G., Depla, C. & Shepherd, M. 'Mental Health Care in the Community: an evaluative study' *Psychological Medicine*. 5, 1975, 372-380.

77. Corney, R.H. 'The Effectiveness of Attached Social Workers in the Management of Depressed Female Patients in General Practice' *Psychological Medicine*. 1984, Monograph Supplement 6, Cambridge University Press.

The Psychogeriatric Patient and the Family

Chris Gilleard

THE PSYCHOGERIATRIC PATIENT

Elderly people with psychiatric disorders arising in or just before old age become psychogeriatric patients when they come into contact with the psychiatric services in their neighbourhood, town or city. But many elderly people with psychiatric disorders are never recognised by primary health care services, or if they are recognised are not referred to a specialist service. The two major syndromes of psychopathology in old age are depression – the most common, affecting some 10-15 per cent of the elderly, and dementia – the second most common, affecting some 5-10 per cent [1]. This chapter focusses upon the elderly with these syndromes, irrespective of their 'contact' status as psychogeriatric patients.

Whilst the prevalence of dementia increases with increasing age, being rare in the sixties, but very common (over 20 per cent) in the eighties and nineties, depressive syndromes show no evidence of a linear increase with increasing age. Indeed, there is a decline in neurotic depressions reported to the psychiatric services in later old age [2]. One direct consequence of this age-related trend in major psychogeriatric syndromes for caregivers, is that the very old are more likely to be widowed, and thus dementia victims will more often have a primary caregiver who is an adult (middle aged) child; in contrast, recognised depressive disorders will affect more individuals at earlier ages, who have a spouse as their principal supporter.

THE SOCIO-DEMOGRAPHIC PATTERNS OF CAREGIVING

According to a recent estimate from the Family Policy Studies Centre [6], estimated costs of family care to the elderly in Britain in 1982/3 lie between £3.7 and £5.3 billions, more than the total cost spent on all health and personal social services for all over 75's. Proportionately more elderly people are cared for now by their families than at the beginning of this century [3]. Nevertheless, the availability of the traditional adult, middle aged daughter/caregiver is likely to be compromised by significant social changes that are occurring in work and marriage.

Figures from North America and Britain demonstrate the rise in the number of married working women, especially in the post-war period [4,5]. The declining ratio of available middle aged children, and the increasing rate of divorce are further trends likely to limit the supply of caregivers to the very elderly [6].

These are very broad trends, indicating possible crises in family support systems over the next 15 to 25 years. What of the present? Several recent studies have described the patterns of support given to the elderly confused which seem to indicate a common distribution of caregiving. Levin, Sinclair and Gorback [7] describe in considerable detail the characteristics of 150 supporters of the elderly confused, the vast majority of whom were either the elderly's children or spouses, with siblings and daughters-in-law providing the principal other type of supporter. A similar survey of 129 supporters of patients referred for psychogeriatric day hospital care [8], obtained similar proportions – 43 per cent children, 38 per cent spouses, the remainder being siblings or daughters-in-law, while George [9], in a large postal survey of dementia supporters, found slightly higher numbers of spouses (54 per cent) than children (34 per cent). This difference may, of course, be due to George's survey focussing on Alzheimer's disease/dementia – thus including middle aged dementia victims more likely to have fit and able spouses.

The pattern of caregiving in all such studies suggests that the principal supporter of the mentally frail elderly will be the spouse, if fit and available. Since men are usually older than their wives, and have a shorter lifespan, this means more wives than husbands act as caregivers. If the person's spouse is unfit, dead or otherwise unavailable, the task of caregiving devolves on the nearest available daughter. Only when daughters are unavailable, does responsibility finally devolve on to sons; the absence of children altogether seems finally to bring in siblings, nieces or occasionally neighbours. This system of caregiver responsibility emphasises the extent to which such caregiving is a solitary, often isolating experience. In Levin's study [7], almost half (44 per cent) of the supporters saw one or less visitors during each week, while in our own study 20 per cent of the supporters received no visitors in the week preceding the interview. Despite the advocacy of shared family caregiving to the elderly mentally infirm by professionals [10], it seems that the usual pattern for many caregivers is an increasingly single-handed duty to a parent or spouse, who is more often than not female. It seems that when the caregiver is male, however, a greater mobilisation of additional caregivers takes place — for example, a greater amount of assistance is expected of wives/daughters-in-law by caregiving sons than is expected of husbands/sons-in-law, who may give little more than a grudging tolerance of their wives' parent-caring involvement [11].

STRESS AND STRAIN AMONG THE SUPPORTERS OF DEMENTING RELATIVES

From the foregoing section, it is unsurprising that caregiving is so often a highly stressful experience. Recent research has attempted to analyse in more detail the factors responsible for amplifying or mitigating these feelings of stress and strain. The table overleaf summarises the potential sources of stress and factors thought to mitigate the stress experience which have been investigated by researchers.

Incontinence, night time disturbance, lapses of personal hygiene, apathy and lack of communication, demands for attention and uncharacteristic anti-social or threatening behaviour have all been identified by different researchers as contributing to the caregiver's experience of stress when looking after the elderly mentally infirm [8,12,13,14, 15]. Impairments of activities of daily living, of mobility and of memory do not seem to be closely related to caregivers' stress [16,17, 18], despite the physical burden of lifting, bathing, transferring; furthermore, length of illness or length of time spent caring does not seem to contribute to increasing stress [8,18]. It seems that caring for a dementia victim causes strains when constant supervision of 'risk' is needed, and when behavioural deficits or disturbances act to enhance the change or loss in the relationship between dementia sufferer and supporter; the progress of the dementia itself, and the progressive physical deterioration do not in themselves determine strain. But it is also clear that factors other than number and type of problems contribute to the experience of stress among carers.

Sex matters. Male carers consistently report higher morale and lower distress — even when the demands are the same [7,8,9,11,18]. Men with dementia seem to be more stressful to look after than women — despite presenting similar problems [8,18]. Older (spouse) carers also have been found to report lower levels of strain than younger carers [8]. Zarit [18], discussing the contrasting position of elderly men looking after their dementing wives, with

TABLE 1

Sources and moderators of stress in supporters

Sources of Stress	Potential Moderators of Stress
1. Positive symptoms of dementia e.g. – dangerous behaviour – aggression – wandering – inappropriate urination/defaecation – turning night into day – making accusations	(a) Quality of past relationship (b) Health and well-being of carer (c) Quantity and quality of support from family and friends (d) Quantity and quality of support from services (e) Sex and relationship of carer (f) Sex and relationship of dependant (g) Number of competing responsibilities (h) Use of coping strategies (i) Age of carer
2. Negative symptoms of dementia e.g. – neglect of personal hygiene – forgetting of actions and intentions – loss of interest and grasp	
3. Relationship problems e.g. – breakdown of marital conversation – loss of person (no longer my mother, my husband) – excessive demands on carer	

elderly women looking after their dementing husbands, suggests that men can 'share' caregiving with formal and informal services more easily, and with less threat to their self-esteem. Horowitz [11] has also suggested that such assistance is generally more forthcoming to male supporters.

Help and assistance from others is less straightforward, as Zarit's study found.

Husband carers were less stressed when they received more formal support; wife carers reported more stress. She argued this was because outside help threatened the wife's socialised sense of caregiving responsibility – while husbands, as one man said to me, see it as 'women's work' in any case. Socialisation experiences may also make 'switching off' harder for female caregivers than for male caregivers, even when relief is available.

Certainly those studies which have not considered the sex of caregiver separately have failed to demonstrate any clear relationship between levels of formal and informal help and caregivers' morale or strain [8,17,18]. Some evidence for the stress-reducing value of home helps [7], and psychogeriatric day care [20], does exist. Both these studies provide a longitudinal perspective on formal support, in contrast to the earlier cross-sectional findings. Before dismissing intervention as of little value, therefore, it is necessary to evaluate services over time.

While external help may play a questionable role in determining the stressfulness of caregiving, the caregiving relationship itself may be of particular importance. Several studies have examined 'closeness', 'intimacy', 'mutuality' and 'reciprocity' as potential mediating factors in the caregiving relationship. With one exception, (Gilhooly [18], using an observer rating of quality of past relationship, found no correlation with morale) these studies have found that positive or close relationships between dependant and carer in the past and present are significantly associated with lower levels of strain on the part of the supporter [21,22]. Klussman et al [23] found a similar relationship when 'closeness' was rated by the supporter, but not when it was rated by another family informant. Although potentially valuable constructs to use when working with families living with dementia, mutuality, reciprocity and closeness require more conceptual clarification.

A more straightforward relationship might be expected from consideration of the supporters' age and health status. Surprisingly little attention has been paid to these variables, however. Self-perceived health status is itself strongly associated with emotional distress and is generally independent of age [24]. Age, we found, tended to be associated with lower levels of reported strain [8]. No studies have determined the objective health status of supporters of dementia sufferers though one might imagine that poorer health would make caregiving more difficult and thus more stressful.

Gilhooly [25] has been the only researcher to directly examine the role of caregivers' coping strategies to their morale. She has described how supporters using behavioural coping strategies (doing things to reduce problems, organising help, etc.) report higher morale than those using cognitive-psychological coping strategies (attempts to modify, deny or otherwise control the meaning of the caregiving experience), while those without obvious coping strategies report the lowest morale. Interestingly, male supporters, she found, more often described behavioural coping strategies – perhaps because as Zarit and Horowitz suggest, other family members and formal services are more willing to respond to the 'plight' of a man looking after a woman.

Although not focussing specifically upon dementia sufferers and their carers, Johnson and Catelona [26], have also presented evidence concerning a typology of coping styles in relation to looking after the elderly. They found adult children often coped by using a variety of *distancing* techniques, either physically reducing the frequency and intensity of contact or psychologically distancing themselves from a parent's emotional needs, while maintaining instrumental caregiving in the form of shopping, cleaning, cooking, etc. Such techniques bear a close resemblance to Gilhooly's 'ignoring' strategy, which she also found associated with higher levels of morale. Less often, but with considerable effectiveness, Johnson and Catelona describe some of their adult child carers employing a social diffusion of care as a form of distancing, enlarging the informal caregiving network and reducing the level of isolating caregiving.

In contrast to adult child carers, spouses were found more often to employ 'enmeshing' strategies – often retreating from other social relationships as a couple (*social regression*) or engaging in *role entrenchment*, where caregiving is accepted as a permanent, full time role that takes precedence over all other social roles, and gives new meaning to the carer's life. Though typically associated with spouses, these researchers note that it may often be employed by adult child carers, as a compensation for failures in other role relationships.

FAMILY INTERVENTION STRATEGIES WITH THE CARERS OF DEMENTIA SUFFERERS

Associated with a growing body of recent research into the complex determinants of strain among supporters of dementia sufferers, has been an increasing interest in intervention programmes to reduce this strain. An implicit assumption – so far untested – behind such interventions is that they will prevent institutionalisation of dementia sufferers, while making the community carers (i.e. spouses or daughters) have a more tolerable life. There has been a growing number of people with dementia being cared for at home, and there has not been a concomitant increase in institutional provision – in

Britain, at least [27]. It is sometimes difficult to understand the positive and negative elements motivating such interventions therefore: to facilitate a caring relationship mutually desired by carer and cared-for, or to enforce a cheaper form of care desired by Health Boards and Local Authorities.

While such motivational (and political) factors should not be lost sight of, there is no denying the value of helping carers care more effectively and with a greater sense of personal esteem. Three elements may be identified in the existing literature on family intervention programmes. Many stress the value of providing knowledge and understanding about dementia, its nature, causes and prognosis, to the caregiving relatives (cf. Lazarus, Stafford, Cooper, Cohler and Dysken, [28]). Others emphasise techniques to improve caregiving management, principally using behavioural analysis and modification techniques [29,31]. Thirdly, some researchers have emphasised the working through of grief reactions and relationship issues, as in bereavement counselling [31]. Much of this work has been in groups, where the element of sharing of experiences has been presumably of added benefit: in general, the studies have been poorly evaluated, and outcome in the single case methodology employed by Pinkston and Linsk [30] has been narrow and short term – given the overall chronicity of the problems in caring for dementia sufferers.

More evaluative research is needed in this area, beyond innovatory programmes to examine the relevance of (a) the three components of intervention, i.e. knowledge and understanding, emotional reactions, and management skills, (b) group versus individual counselling of relatives and (c) the knowledge gained about the determinants and complexities of caregiving strain to effective family intervention. Finally, and I believe most importantly, we need to come to a clearer understanding of our goals in this area.

THE DEPRESSED ELDERLY PERSON AND THE FAMILY CONTEXT

Much of the previous sections reflects the unique circumstances of families who have a relative suffering from dementia. The 'patient' may seem to disappear, and the client becomes the carer. I believe this is necessarily so, since dementia reflects the very loss of self and agency which leads others to take over responsibility for the dementing person's household, his or her social roles, and personal maintenance. In depressive conditions, even when delusions of poverty or intestinal decay are evidenced, such a loss of agency and self is absent, and the person's needs, distress or demands come over more individualistically. Thus, while the community needs of the non-dementing elderly psychiatric patient have been recognised for some considerable time (e.g. Colwell and Post [32]) there has been little sustained clinical research interest in the family context of old age depressions, anxiety states or paraphrenic disorders.

Depression in old age can be a chronic or relapsing disorder [2,33, 34], often under-recognised by family doctors [35,36] and under-treated both psychologically and pharmacologically [37]. This latter study demonstrated that during a 15 year follow-up of community-survey identified elderly psychiatric patients, only eight of 43 neurotic patients received formal psychiatric help; only 1.2 per cent of the population were prescribed anti-depressants though 20 per cent received anti-anxiety drugs, 19 per cent anti-psychotic drugs and a staggering 37.4 per cent sedative-hypnotics.

Given the low level of intervention generally, it is hardly surprising that little research has examined the role and impact of the family in old age depression. What research there is tends not to emphasise a significant role for the family in aetiology or prognosis, however. Garside, Kay and Roth [38], found a dimension of social isolation unrelated to functional psychopathology, though social isolation does seem to contribute to hospital admission [37,39]. Murphy [40] found very little difference between her normal and depressed elderly subjects in the numbers experiencing major difficulties with marital and family relationships (3 per cent and 6 per cent only). This contrasts sharply with the very large differences in severe life events, and major problems over health and housing, distinguishing her elderly depressed subjects from the controls. While she found the presence of a 'confidant' reduced elderly people's vulnerability to depression, she felt this reflected more upon life-long personality traits of warmth and the capacity for intimacy – a finding supported by such earlier studies as those by Garside et al. [38] and Vispo [41].

Families do not, therefore, seem to be a significant source of depression to the elderly unless their health is affected, or they are lost to the person through death. This latter source of grief and potential depression has provided the basis for one of the very few studies examining the impact of an elderly depressed relative on the family. Bowling [42], in a study of 215 widowed elderly and their principal supporting relative, found that only 15 per cent of the relatives of the non-depressed widowed described their life as having been significantly affected; 41 per cent of the relatives of the depressed widowed did so. Like many of the studies of dementia patients' relatives, she also found that responsibility for practical and emotional support focussed narrowly upon one particular close relative.

FAMILY INTERVENTION AND FUNCTIONAL PSYCHIATRIC DISORDERS IN OLD AGE

The sparsity of documentation about the effects of the family on the course and outcome of depression and other non-dementing conditions, as well as the absence of research on the reactions of family members to their relatives' condition, is reflected in the paucity of family intervention studies. Occasional clinical cases have been described in the behaviour therapy/modification literature involving modifying spouse interactions (e.g. Davies [43], Pinkston and Linsk [30]), but these have been short term, limited focus interventions, which must be seen against the probable background of chronic psychological problems typically found in non-dementing elderly psychiatric patients.

The extent to which depression is under-recognised and under-treated, is conceptualised within biological/endogenous or intrapsychic terms, and is a publicly quiet affair, probably explains the lack of research attention paid to family intervention studies. There is possibly more research on the impact of pets on the emotional state of the elderly than of family counselling and intervention, though one may well speculate on the long term stresses on spouses of chronically depressed elderly people, and the likely demands on middle aged children, induced by 'agoraphobic' elderly parents. At present, research provides few points on how best to meet the needs of families involved in supporting an elderly psychiatrically distressed person who is mentally alert and able.

CONCLUSIONS

What has research found in the area of mental illness in old age and the family? First, it is increasingly clear that caring for the vast majority of dementia sufferers in the community is creating an enormous burden, whether measured in economic or psychological terms. It is an increasing cause of minor psychiatric morbidity, and for many women a lifetime of unending caring. This terrible stress lies in important ways in the very nature of dementia itself, and the drastic and insidious way it erodes the person, and thus the relationship between husband and wife, or parent and child.

A greater appreciation of the emotional distress and reactions among carers is needed and reports such as those by Lazarus et al [29], Barnes, Raskind, Scott and Murphy [44], Tevsink and Mahler [31], can help alert professionals to these issues. Equally, studies by Greene et al [14] and Gilleard et al [8] help alert professionals to the likely problems carers can face, and the types of problems they find particularly difficult to handle.

Studies demonstrating the stress-reducing value of home help services, and psychogeriatric daycare [7,20], provide support to press for the greater availability of these services. Equally, reports stressing the family perspective in psychogeriatrics provide valuable direction to workers in this field [10].

The lack lies in the level of precision. We know too little about what sort of interventions, how to make them, who benefits from them and why they sometimes break down. We need to know much more about the failures of interventions, and clinician/researchers need to be as willing to publish innovations that fall flat as they are to boast of their successes.

Finally, we lack much knowledge about the impact of chronic depression and other functional psychiatric disorders on the family. As Colwell and Post [32] wrote over 25 years ago:

> '...beyond vague impressions, very little is known about the therapeutic effectiveness of community care for elderly people with psychological illness or difficulties.'

The situation is a little clearer as regards dementia, but remains the same for the functional illnesses – primarily because of a lack of research, which like public attention, has been focussed upon the slow 'epidemic of dementia', a costlier business than dysphoria, depression and despair.

References

1. Kay, D.W.K. & Bergmann, K. *'Epidemiology of Mental Disorders Amongst the Aged in the Community'*. In Birren, J.E. & Sloane, R.B. (Eds.) *Handbook of Mental Health and Aging.* Prentice-Hall, Englewood Cliffs, N.J., 1980, 34-56.

2. Kay, D.W.K. 'The Depressions and Neuroses of Later Life'. In Granville-Grossman, K. (Ed.) *Recent Advances in Clinical Psychiatry.* Vol.2., Churchill-Livingstone, Edinburgh, 1976, 52-80.

3. D.H.S.S. *Growing Older.* HMSO, London, 1981.

4. Brody, E.M. 'Women in the Middle, and Family Help to Older People' *The Gerontologist.* 23, 1981, 471-480.

5. Joshi, H., Layard, R. & Owen, S. *Why are More Women Working in Britain?* Centre for Labour Economics, London School of Economics, June 1983.

6. Family Policy Studies Centre *The Forgotten Army: Family Care and Elderly People.* Briefing paper, The Family Policy Studies Centre, Park Road, London N.W.1, 1984.

7. Levin, E., Sinclair, I. & Garbach, P. *The Supporters of Confused Elderly Persons at Home.* DHSS Commissioned Research Project, Vols. 1,2 & 3, 1983. National Institute for Social Work Research Unit, London.

8. Gilleard, C.J., Gilleard, E., Whittick, J. & Gledhill, K. 'Caring for the Elderly Mentally Infirm at Home: a survey of the supporters' *Journal of Epidemiology and Community Health.* 38, 1984, 319-325.

9. George, L.K. 'The Burden of Caregiving: how much? what kinds? for whom?' *Center Reports on Advances in Research.* Vol.8, No 1984, Duke University Center for the Study of Aging and Human Development.

10. Watt, G.M. 'A Family Oriented Approach to Community Care for the Elderly Mentally Infirm' *Nursing Times.* 78 (37), 1982, 1545-1548.

11. Horowitz, A. 'Sons and Daughters as Caregivers to Older Parents: differences in role performance and consequences'. Paper presented at the 34th Annual Scientific Meeting of the Gerontological Society of America, Toronto, Canada, November 1981.

12. Sanford, J.R.A. 'Tolerance of Debility in Elderly Dependents by Supporters at Home: its significance for hospital practice' *British Medical Journal.* 3, 75, 1975, 471-475.

13. Machin, E. *A Survey of the Behaviour of the Elderly and their Supporters at Home.* Unpublished MSc. thesis, University of Birmingham, U.K., 1980.

14. Greene, J.G., Smith, R., Gardiner, M. & Timbury, G.C. 'Measuring Behavioural Disturbance of Elderly Demented Patients in the Community and its Effects on Relatives: a factor analytic study' *Age and Ageing.* 11, 1982, 121-126.

15. Gilhooly. M.L.M. 'The Social Aspect of Dementia'. In Hanley, I.G. & Hodge, J. (Eds.) *Psychological Approaches to the Care of the Elderly.* Croom-Helm, Ltd., London, 1984.

16. Gilleard, C.J. 'Problems Posed for Supporting Relatives of Geriatric and Psychogeriatric Day Patients' *Acta Psychiatrica Scandinavica.* 70, 1984a, 198-208.

17. Zarit, S.H., Reever, K.E. & Bach-Peterson, J. 'Relatives of the Impaired Aged: correlates of feelings of burden' *The Gerontologist.* 20, 1980, 649-655.

18. Gilhooly, M.L.M. 'The Impact of Caregiving on Caregivers: factors associated with the psychological well being of people supporting a dementing relative in the community' *British Journal of Medical Psychology.* 1984(b).

19. Zarit, J.M. 'Family Roles, Social Supports and their Relation to Caregivers' Burden'. Paper presented at the Western Psychological Association's annual meeting, Sacramento, California, July 1982.

20. Gilleard, C.J. (in press) 'Impact of Psychogeriatric Day Care on the Patients' Supporting Relatives' *Health Bulletin.* Edinburgh, 1985.

21. Hirschfield, M.J. 'Families Living and Coping with the Cognitively Impaired'. In Archer Copp, L. (Ed.) *Recent Advances in Nursing No.2. Care of the ageing.* Edinburgh, Churchill-Livingstone, 1981.

22. Horowitz, A. & Shindelman, L.W. 'Reciprocity and Affection: past influences on current caregiving'. Paper presented at the 34th Annual Scientific Meeting of the Gerontological Society of America, Toronto, Canada, November 1981.

23. Klussman, D., Bruder, J., Lauter, H. & Luders, I. 'Relationships Between Patients and their Relatives in Illness of Extreme Old Age' (in German). Teilprojekt Alb, Sonderforschungsbereich 115 der Deutschen Forschungsgerneinschaft, Hamburg, 1981.

24. Murray, J., Dunn, G. & Tarnapolsky, A. 'Self Assessment of Health: an exploration of the effects of physical and psychological symptoms' *Psychological Medicine*. 12, 1982, 371-378.

25. Gilhooly, M.L.M. 'The Social Dimensions of Senile Dementia'. Paper presented at the British Psychological Society Annual Conference, Aberdeen, March 1980.

26. Johnson, C.L. & Catelona, D.J. 'A Longitudinal Study of Family Supports to the Impaired Elderly' *The Gerontologist*. 23, 1983, 612-618.

27. Gilleard, C.J. *Living with Dementia: Community Care of the Elderly Infirm*. 1984(b) Croom Helm Ltd., London.

28. Lazarus, L.W., Stafford, B., Cooper, K., Cohler, B. & Dyksen, M. 'A Pilot Study of an Alzheimer Patient's Relatives Discussion Group' *The Gerontologist*. 21, 1981, 253-358.

29. Haley, W.E. 'A Family-Behavioural Approach to the Treatment of the Cognitively Impaired Elderly' *The Gerontologist*. 23, 1983, 18-20.

30. Pinkston, E.M. & Linsk, N.L. 'Behavioural Family Intervention with the Impaired Elderly' *The Gerontologist*. 24, 1984, 576-583.

31. Tevsink, J.P. & Mahler, S. 'Helping Families Cope with Alzheimer's Disease' *Hospital and Community Psychiatry*. 35, 1984, 152-156.

32. Colwell, C. & Post, F. 'Community Needs of Elderly Psychiatric patients' *British Medical Journal*. August 22nd, 1959, 214-217.

33. Post, F. 'Management and Nature of Depressive Illness in Late Life: a follow-through study' *British Journal of Psychiatry*. 121, 1972, 393-404.

34. Murphy, E. 'The Prognosis of Depression in Old Age' *British Journal of Psychiatry*. 142, 1983, 111-119.

35. Williamson, J., Stokoe, I.H., Gray, S., et al. 'Old People at Home: their unreported needs' *Lancet*. i, 1964, 1117-1120.

36. Waxman, H.M. & Carner, E.A. 'Physicians' Recognition, Diagnosis and Treatment of Mental Disorders in Elderly Medical Patients' *The Gerontologist*. 24, 1984, 593-597.

37. Neilsen, J., Homma, A. & Biorn-Henriksen, T. 'Follow Up 15 Years After a Geriatric-Psychiatric Prevalence Study in Samso. Part 1. Geriatric Services' *Comprehensive Psychiatry*. 18, 1977, 533-544.

38. Garside, R.F., Kay, D.W.K. & Roth, M. 'Old Age Mental Disorders in Newcastle-Upon-Tyne: III a factorial study of medical psychiatric and social characteristics' *British Journal of Psychiatry*. III, 1965, 939-946.

39. Kay, D.W.K., Beamish, P. & Roth, M. 'Some Medical and Social Characteristics of Elderly People under State Care: a comparison of geriatric wards, mental hospitals and welfare homes' *The Sociological Review Monographs*. No.5, 1962, 173-193.

40. Murphy, E. 'Social Origins of Depression in Old Age' *British Journal of Psychiatry*. 141, 1982, 135-142.

41. Vispo, R.H. 'Pre-Morbid Personality in the Functional Psychoses of the senium' *Journal of Mental Science*. 108, 1962, 790-799.

42. Bowling, A. 'Caring for the Elderly Widowed – the Burden on their Supporters' *British Journal of Social Work*. No.14, 1983, 435-455.

43. Davies, A.D.M. 'Neither Wife nor Widow' *Behaviour Research and Therapy*. 19, 1981, 449-451.

44. Barnes, R., Raskind, M., Scott, M. & Murphy, C. 'Problems of Families Caring for Alzheimer Patients: use of a support group' *Journal of the American Geriatrics Society*. 29, 1981, 80-85.

The Effects of Mental Illness on the Family: Social Work Practitioner's View

Ruth Smith and Gill West

INTRODUCTION

> 'Schizophrenia is a fearful illness. Having a son with schizophrenia and a husband who died of cancer, I would choose cancer every time [1].
>
> Living with someone who has manic depression means each day is like a tightrope. Always having to watch what you say and worry of how depressed they are. Constantly wondering if it's safe to leave them alone today. Feeling angry and yet trying to understand – sometimes it just gets too much to cope with.'
>
> (Case History)

As social workers in the field of mental health we acknowledge that there is a wide spectrum of disorders called mental illness, varying from the milder neuroses, from which we more or less all suffer, to the severely disabling psychotic illnesses requiring varying lengths of in and/or outpatient psychiatric treatment. We wish to address ourselves specifically to the problems of the families of patients who have been diagnosed by psychiatrists as suffering from a mental illness. We recognise that, already, we touch on an area of continuing, though increasingly less sharply polarised, debate concerning the matter of the selection of patients for psychiatric treatment [2, 3, 4].

This article is less concerned with chronic organic disorders of the elderly or the psychiatric illnesses associated with adolescence. We tend to be concerned, largely, with the families of those who have been diagnosed as suffering from chronic mental illness, with the emphasis being on those who suffer from psychotic illness, and accept that there will be features, relating to the effects of psychiatric illness, which are common to a wide variety of disability. In the battle for scarce welfare resources we believe that this particular group of psychiatric patients and their families is particularly disadvantaged.

During the last 25 years there have been significant changes in the treatment of the mentally ill, particularly in the availability and use of effective psychotropic drugs and the increased informality in the organisation of psychiatric hospitals. However, we are concerned that despite the expanding numbers of people who feel able to seek psychiatric help, the considerable media exposure of the plight of the mentally ill, the consistent government policy in favour of community rather than institutional care of psychiatric patients, there has been little concerted effort to support families. We do not assume that families carry a greater burden than the sufferer nor that community care should be concentrated within the family, but wish simply to highlight the problems experienced by members of the families of those suffering from a mental illness. The Parliamentary Select Committee chaired by Renee Short noted that care of the mentally ill in the community 'cannot be done on the cheap; it is no good imagining that community care will save money; it means providing supporting services for those mentally disabled people who currently have little contact with statutory services, *and for their families*' [5].

We wish in this article to consider (a) the effects on the family occasioned by the ways in which help in dealing with psychiatric symptoms within a family is sought; (b) the intra-familial aspects of mental illness; (c) the extra-familial features; and (d) the main facets of social work provision which we regard as pertinent in working with the mentally ill and their families.

HELP SEEKING

The ways in which families and patients begin to recognise illness and seek help have relevance to service provision both in the statutory and voluntary field and to the severity of the problems families carry. Brown et al [6], Creer and Wing [7] and Davies [8] have all highlighted the fact that families of the mentally ill tend to disregard those symptoms which develop gradually. Families seem to make considerable adjustments to their daily lives and in their expectations of quality of life. It seems that families generally regard the matter of accommodating the needs of the mentally ill member as a duty [9]. Over a period of years, far reaching changes in lifestyle may result such that, for example, relatives may not feel able to leave the sufferer alone for fear of her/his harming her/himself.

Stigma plays a part both in seeking and maintaining contact with the psychiatric service. Families and patients continue to be reluctant to face the prospect of becoming consumers of the psychiatric services and frequently explain their difficulties in terms of physical illness or trauma, apparently in accordance with their view of what the general practitioner may be willing to listen to. There appears, too, to be a good deal of variation in the ability of GPs to identify psychiatric symptoms, perhaps as a result of such a tendency [4]. This negative view of mental illness, shared by relatives and, it may be reasonably assumed, by GPs as well as neighbours and employers, while being a continuing feature in the lives of the mentally ill, may be particularly significant at the help seeking stage.

Close relatives feel guilt: 'What did I do wrong?' asks the mother of a son who suffers from schizophrenia [1]. Fairly unsubstantiated theories of causation were prevalent in the 1960's. Laing and Esterson [10], concerned with focussing exclusively on past childhood and family relationships and current family dynamics, tended to exacerbate the existing troubles of the families of the mentally ill. Though Laing talked largely of the plight of the patient suffering from schizophrenia, his widely read view of madness as a sane response to insane family relationships naturally adversely affected the provision of supportive services that relatives could draw on to care for their ill member [9].

The notion of success being associated with keeping a patient in the community and failure as an admission to psychiatric hospital, may further delay the help seeking process not only within families but on the part of GPs and social workers [11]. Goldberg, Huxley and Williams [4, 12], indicate that psychiatric morbidity may be fairly seriously under-detected by community based professionals and, though this undetected group may fall at the less severe end of the psychiatric symptom spectrum, it may represent a fair measure of treatable, but untreated depression.

Help seeking, not surprisingly, is more prompt in families where conflict is evident [13]. There may, too, be class differences in the process of seeking help. Class IV and V tend to seek help from members of the family network, while Classes 1 and 11 may be more inclined to confide in friends, acquaintances, support groups and professionals [1]. Howitz [14] notes that there are considerable differences in help seeking related to sex, men discussing their problems with, on average, only one person outside the nuclear family while women make help seeking contacts with on average 4.5 people outside the family. Chester [15] suggests that the traditionally dependent female role makes help seeking more acceptable for women. Other factors such as distance from clinic or health centre and knowledge of the nature of help will also play a significant part.

The pathway to psychiatric treatment is therefore complex and fraught with difficulty. Delay in seeking help may be positively disadvantageous in terms of the course of illness, family relationships and the burden of care.

THE HOSPITAL BASED PSYCHIATRIC SERVICE

The psychiatric hospital continues to be the main focus of help seeking within the psychiatric service [16] despite predictions to the contrary in the early and mid 70's [17]. The precipitate closing of large mental hospitals in England is not yet in evidence in Scotland. The relatives of the sufferer from mental illness thus relate to the staff of an acute admission ward or outpatient clinic which is part of a large institution, the main feature of which is the dominant position held by the medical profession. Reading [1] found that relatives tended to be passive in their acceptance of the almost exclusively medical and hospital focus of the service. Some, however, did feel that they as relatives may be viewed by staff as 'being a bit of a nuisance', and the doctors as one mother said 'don't really want to know about your ideas'. Creer and Wing [7] noted that patients' families tended to be undemanding of the services, while Reading found that one or two relatives in his study who had attempted to challenge the diagnosis or treatment regime were left feeling angry that their opinions had been ignored. The sense of alienation, documented in the literature, that relatives may feel in relating to the services, can be compounded by the possibility that friends and acquaintances change in their attitudes to close relatives following the psychiatric admission of a member of their family. Miles [9] states that families who have a mentally ill member experience an overall reduction in social contacts. Creer and Wing [7], too, point out that when relatives do overcome the difficulties of inviting friends to the house in which a mentally ill relative lives, they often find that there are not many friends who come back. The resultant isolation of relatives may be further exacerbated by the difficulty that psychiatric professional workers have in communicating with relatives, restricted as they inevitably are by their code of confidentiality [17].

It is easy to see how professional workers come to focus their treatment and thus indeed their emotional commitment to 'success' on the patient to the exclusion of the family. The difficulties experienced by people suffering from mental illness evoke feelings of helplessness and much sympathy among caring workers. In their attempts to ameliorate this suffering, workers may over-identify with the patient and come to see the family in a negative context. It is a difficult and demanding task to simultaneously boost the strengths and coping abilities of patient and close relatives.

First admission to hospital is a significant event in the pathway to psychiatric treatment and may be the single most important step in defining a person with problems as a psychiatric patient. Bean [19] found that one outpatient (referred in a crisis situation) in three becomes an inpatient. Hospital admission as engineered by immediate relatives may involve a good deal of subterfuge on their part and considerable pressure on the patient who mostly believes that there is nothing wrong with him/her [9]. There is some evidence to suggest that patients coming to see a psychiatrist for the first time may not know that it is a psychiatrist that he/she will be seeing, and that GPs and relatives may collude for a variety of reasons in the patient's reluctance to face this reality [20]. One must assume that by perpetuating the apparently accepted norm that in some way 'Psychiatrist' and 'Mental Hospital' are words from which the patient needs to be protected, professional workers and relatives contribute to the continuing stigma attached to these words and their concatenation.

Individual accounts of hospital admission by patients indicate that, as yet, professional workers have not found a satisfactory way of smoothing the path of the patient and his/her relatives in seeking admission to hospital at times of crisis [21]. New mental health legislation [Mental Health (Scotland) Act 1984] with an increased emphasis on the civil rights aspects of compulsory admission, may offer the psychiatric patient a more open and honest service in relation to detention in hospital. It is unlikely however, in itself, in giving the patient and his/her next of kin a more effective voice at times of acute phases of illness, to offer a less painful route to treatment. The increased legal responsibilities of the Mental Health Officer offer social work departments the opportunity to provide an advocacy service alongside a sympathetic understanding and management of family dilemma at times of compulsory admission, providing that additional staffing resources are available for this area of work.

Relatives do appear to find difficulty in relating to the large mental hospital ward. Reading [1] found that relatives were confused by the numbers of ward based staff to whom they spoke. There would seem to be a case for multi-disciplinary teams adopting a key worker approach to this problem, such that one designated member of staff is responsible for relating to family members. Particular difficulties in this matter may be experienced by relatives and patients who live some distance from the hospital [22].

Given all these difficulties, it is crucial that the relatives of the mentally ill do not become alienated from their ill relative by virtue of admission at inpatient or at outpatient referral stage.

INTRA-FAMILIAL ASPECTS

Agnes Miles [9] states:

'The acceptance or rejection of psychiatric patients by their families is a complex issue. The picture that emerges from most studies is that of families willing to accommodate and to receive back the patient from hospital.'

While we do not wish to indicate that such an acceptance always constitutes a burden of care for the family, it is clear from the work of Creer and Wing [7] and Grad and Sainsbury [23], that there is a significant element of disruption in household routine, reduction of income and opportunities for social life, as well as an increase in emotional stress. An indication of the extent of stress may be the incidence of marital breakdown. Brown [24] notes that the rate of separation and divorce among patients suffering from schizophrenia may be as much as three times higher than for the general population. These findings have been repeated in American Studies [25, 26]. There is of course no clear picture of specific cause and effect. Thus life events such as childbirth, bereavement, separation and divorce, unemployment and retirement all play a significant part in triggering mental illness [27, 28, 24]. From the study of short stay psychiatric patients [29], it seems that many have begun to lose their ties with spouses and family members before they become long stay inpatients. While some of the explanation for this finding may be related to 'down-ward drift' [30] and to the likelihood that those outpatients without kin at home are more likely to be deemed at risk and therefore more likely to be admitted to an acute bed, there is, from our practical experience, much to reinforce the notion that mental illness is a causal factor in marital breakdown. Many spouses do struggle for many years to maintain a marital relationship which, in the end, may founder because of the severity of illness experienced by his/her partner.

Children too appear to be significantly affected by the mental illness of one or both parents. Rutter et al [30] found nearly twice as many examples of continuing emotional and behavioural disturbance in such children when compared with class room controls. Cooper et al [32] found that 45 per cent of psychiatric patients' children suffered from psychiatric disorders as against

26 per cent of children in a control group. Rutter proposed that it is not the severity of the mental illness *per se* which produces adverse effects but the concomitant features of illness, e.g. erratic parenting and the increased responsibility children may have to assume to compensate for illness in one of their parents. In practice we are aware of this area of largely unmet need in relation to the provision of domiciliary or other compensatory support for children of mentally ill adults. While it seems that the children of parents suffering from psychotic disorders were less strikingly affected than in Rutter's study, Rice, Ekdahl and Miller [35], Newman [36], Cooper et al [32] have noted several serious problems and stressful situations for such children. Garmezy [37] notes the difficulties for children of psychotic parents in terms of the inconsistency of parenting, parents often not being able to offer even basic physical care at times of acute illness. Children, too, are not immune from the effects of stigma associated with the illness of their parent and this alongside the anxiety which distressing psychotic symptoms may arouse, will inevitably contribute to a reduction in life prospects for this group of children.

The work of Brown [38], Leff and Vaughan [39] in relation to the index of High and Low Expressed Emotion of relatives of patients suffering from schizophrenia, has thrown some interesting light on the complex matter of relapse of illness. Patients who spend more than 35 hours per week in face to face contact with those relatives assessed 'High E.E.' have a much higher relapse rate than those in the same circumstances with 'Low E.E.' relatives. These findings are independent of regular drug therapy. There are of course clear implications for the provision of day, evening and weekend 'care' for the person suffering from schizophrenia living with a high E.E. relative. Leff points out that often relatives as well as sufferers are lacking in the motivation necessary to use available facilities. It may be necessary to use other means to loosen the ties of what may have become a destructively symbiotic relationship between sufferer and high E.H. relative.

It is often difficult and sometimes impossible to live with a relative who is suffering from a severe mental illness. On purely humanitarian grounds, professional workers need to be aware, and need to acknowledge to relatives their awareness of the stresses of care.

EXTRA FAMILIAL FEATURES

Reading [1] gained the impression that middle income groups were less materially affected by having a member of the family suffering from mental illness than were low income groups. While this may appear to be a tautological statement, the picture is rather more complex, involving a number of inter-related features.

The downward drift described by Goldberg and Morrison [30] refers to the way that people who develop mental illness drift into a lower social class. Brown et al [38] noted that stress specific to the working class environment could be causal in relation to depression. The differential labelling and differential treatment described by Miles [9] gives some indication that working class patients are more likely to be diagnosed mentally ill, and less likely to leave the role of the mental patient, than those from middle class backgrounds. The families of the mentally ill are more likely to be exposed to the detrimental effects of low income.

Cartwright and O'Brien [40] highlight the fact that it is the middle class N.H.S. patient who is better able to make effective use of the service. It is a fair assumption that such is also the case for the psychiatric patient. In view of the clearly documented downward spiral of deprivation among psychiatric patients it would seem that there needs to be more determined efforts on the part of professional workers to attempt to redress this imbalance.

Not only is there evidence of downward mobility implying acceptance of a lower income; studies also reveal a higher rate of unemployment among the mentally ill. The lack of a job in itself brings a reduction in self esteem and an increase in financial difficulty producing considerable stress on family and individual. Meacher [41] and Hill [42] link unemployment and the onset of psychiatric symptoms. Brown et al [6] found that while employers may be sympathetic to one psychiatric hospital admission, after multiple admissions nearly two-thirds of their sample were unemployed. At times of high unemployment, those suffering from mental illness are clearly further disadvantaged in terms of finding appropriate work. The less prestigious jobs which may have been available previously are no longer open to those suffering from psychiatric illness. The loss of confidence and real ability to concentrate, which may follow an acute phase of illness and treatment, together with the scarcity of employment, may mean that the sufferer needs to spend a good deal of his/her working life in a sheltered occupation which offers only basic income, a circumstance which may produce effects on the family similar to those experienced by the long term unemployed.

While Brown and Harris [43] have indicated that employment outside the home may be preventive in terms of depression in women, for a number of people suffering from chronic mental illness the pressure of open employment may be too great. For people in this situation self esteem needs to be bolstered in other ways.

Another factor which has been suggested as of importance is housing. However, no clear relationship has been documented between the kind of housing that one occupies and the onset of mental illness [44], although Richman [45] postulated that living in a flat rather than a house may be connected with depression in women who have children under five years. Difficulties in relating satisfactorily to neighbours and the wider community is often an observed feature of the lives of those who are mentally ill and their families. In our experience, the nature of such problems does not seem to be related to the kind of housing nor necessarily to the kind of neighbourhood. Neighbours who initially respond negatively to the mental illness label can be helped by professional workers to adopt a more tolerant attitude. A variety of kinds of housing should be available to meet individual and family needs as far as possible. The difficulties associated with poor quality housing, overcrowding, dampness and lack of facilities will be a source of stress for the mentally ill and their families as they are for all of us.

Poor housing, reduced chances of employment, single parent status and low income can conspire along with the stigma of the label of mental illness, to reduce life chances. This inevitably exacerbates problems of family relationships.

SOCIAL WORK

The tongue in cheek prototype of the social worker provided by Barbara Hudson [46] may raise an eyebrow or two among our colleagues from other disciplines:

> '........can do casework and group work according to a variety of different models; he is an administrator and a planner; he is a political campaigner; and his education has prepared him to read critically, to be articulate and to be able to conceptualise his work and generalise appropriately from his experience. He is knowledgeable about psychology, sociology and social policy.......and he can develop specialised skills for work in the psychiatric services.'

Goldberg and Huxley [4] present a less rosy picture:

> 'The Social Work role in relation to the mentally ill patient has in most local authorities become stagnant, and the emphasis has remained

upon outdated methods of intervention which has led to the atrophy of skill development.'

While our only quarrel with the first quotation might be that this super-worker appears to be necessarily male, we do acknowledge that the real picture of the typical social worker lies somewhere between the two extremes. It is indeed the case that local authorities' personal social services departments appear to have become concerned almost exclusively with statutory Child Care work [4]. The debates concerned with specialism v. genericism v. 'patch' have not significantly improved the overall specialist service to the mentally ill and their families. The lack of specialist post qualifying training opportunities is as much a function of the dearth of demand for such training among generically trained staff as it is the result of the financial restrictions placed on local authorities [47]. The continued trend for post qualifying training being that of an 'on the job' kind inhibits the social work contribution in the care of the mentally ill and thus reduces the credibility of the profession *vis a vis* other professional disciplines working in this field. It is to be hoped that the training of Approved Mental Health Officers might begin to help alleviate this problem.

It is quite evident that social workers have a role in joining other professionals at primary care level in helping to identify psychiatric symptoms which might best be treated by professional psychiatric workers. The perennial dilemma within personal social services departments is that of attempting to make a choice between working in a preventative way with larger numbers of patients who are not yet in contact with the psychiatric services, or in an intensive way with the smaller numbers of patients and families who are attempting to cope with the effects of a diagnosed psychiatric disorder. However, the reality of the demand for a social work service at (a) acute admission stage and (b) in enabling the rehabilitation of chronic patients, tends to mean that social workers in mental health are firstly concentrated in hospital (in Scotland) and secondly may tend to take up a fairly traditional casework approach with individual sufferers. In doing so, one suspects that social workers collude in the apparent alienation of relatives from patients. In apparently trivial yet subtle ways, by for example addressing patients on first meetings by first name, by having an immediate and informed understanding of symptoms which relatives may have been battling to tolerate and understand for many years, the social worker along with medical and nursing colleagues may unwittingly reinforce the family's sense of guilt and hopelessness and may undermine their confidence in dealing with the ill family member. The relief that relatives feel in seeking and finding psychiatric treatment may be overwhelming and the services must be mindful that they do not collude in the family's understandable tendency to want to hand over the whole problem. It is a clear social work remit to enable relatives to understand the organisational structure of the services and the best means of communicating with the appropriate professional workers.

Social workers have a part to play in helping relatives deal with the practicalities of hospital admission, in protecting property, ensuring that the patient's welfare rights are met and in helping the patient maintain links with home and community. The care and domiciliary support of patients' children, who will need to have the opportunity to voice or express their fears and will often need help to understand their parents' behaviour, is properly the work of the social worker. In the case of compulsory admission the widened powers of the Mental Health Officer emphasise the need for the social worker as advocate and protector of civil rights. Social workers need to be aware of the difficulties in assessing optimum length of inpatient stay and in enabling relatives and patient prepare for a return to the community. In the case of those patients who have lost their family ties, the social work agency and clinical team becomes almost surrogate family, a circumstance which has considerable implications for social work and multi-disciplinary team cohesion.

It seems to be the case, from the work of Leff [48], that a supportive family network offers the sufferer of schizophrenia and perhaps to a lesser extent the sufferer of depression the better chance of survival outside hospital. This kind of network can be encouraged and nurtured by professional intervention. It is not that social workers should be seeking to encourage relatives to tolerate the intolerable in terms of living with a person who is suffering from psychotic illness; it is rather a plea that relatives be adequately supported by sympathetic counselling, residential relief (not automatically via an admission to psychiatric hospital), day time separation by means of the patient having either paid employment or imaginative day time occupation, and evening social outlets for patients and relatives either together or separately. While it seems to be true that many relatives give up the struggle to live with their ill relatives it is almost certainly desirable on purely humanitarian grounds that relatives are helped to maintain some manageable level of contact. While social workers may traditionally be involved in marital or separation work with couples, in hard pressed social work agencies the importance of supporting relatives may be under-estimated.

The problems experienced by the children of the mentally ill become a particularly painful area of work for the social worker whose focus may be divided between the best interests of the child and the mental health of the parent. While the research shows there are adverse effects on children who live with a mentally ill parent there are no clear guidelines for the social worker working with individual cases in weighing up a series of imponderables regarding how best these effects can be reduced. It is important that the social worker deal effectively with the practice philosophies of other disciplines in these particularly difficult family situations and that mentally ill parents are not subjected to judgmental decisions made on the basis of mental illness alone.

Though research does not yet indicate clear causal links between accommodation and mental illness the need for the right balance between privacy and social contact for the patient suffering from schizophrenia is one that must be considered in helping a patient live outside hospital. Social workers need to be campaigning for the provision of alternative accommodation for patients who cannot or do not want for a variety of reasons to live with their relatives. Such accommodation needs to vary from affording the client the opportunity to live an entirely independent life, to long term hostel-type accommodation. The provision of such accommodation should take into account family ties as appropriate. The matching of client to suitable accommodation is a complicated task. Community care which includes real support for relatives has not expanded greatly since the study by Grad and Sainsbury [23], but there have been notable developments, most of which have not cost the statutory authorities large sums of money. In the North East of Scotland one can point to the Friendship Club [49], Stepping Stones [50] (Aberdeen) and the Pillar Project [51] as moves in the direction of helping the consumer take some responsibility for the organisation and running of the support giving service. The National Schizophrenia Fellowship at national and local level has clearly offered relatives of schizophrenia sufferers an effective political voice as well as ongoing support and guidance. More initiatives on the part of housing associations alongside the development of collaboration between local health board and social services staff should increase the variety of supported accommodation. Local mental health associations have grown in stature and credibility in recent years and continue to wrestle with problems of promoting programmes relating to good mental health through the provision of alternatives to statutory services.

We do not suggest that community care should be exclusively family care, nor that family care should be in any way an alternative to the provision of a variety of support-giving networks in the community. We do propose that support and help for relatives be incorporated in such schemes. Relatives have, since 'Laingian' times, had a bad name in terms of treatment of psychiatric disorder. It is appropriate that their considerable needs are recognised and met if we are realistically to enhance our efforts to meet the needs of those suffering from mental illness.

We hope that the recommendations of the Short Report will not be shelved on the grounds of lack of finance but that there will be a more determined effort to shift resources in favour of community based provision designed to lighten the load of sufferer and family.

Notes and References

1. Reading, P. *Mental Illness and the Family*. Unpublished dissertation, Brunel University, January 1983.

2. Szasz, T. *The Myth of Mental Illness*. Harper, New York, 1961.
   Szasz, T. *The Manufacture of Madness*. Routledge, London, 1971.

3. Laing, R.D. *The Divided Self*. Tavistock, London, 1959.
   Laing, R.D. *The Self and Others*. Tavistock, London, 1961.
   Laing, R.D. *The Politics of Experience*. Penguin, Harmondsworth, 1967.

4. Goldberg, D. & Huxley, P. *Mental Illness in the Community*. Tavistock Publications, London, 1980.

5. *Short Report*. House of Commons Social Services Committee, HMSO, 1985.

6. Brown, G., Bone, M., Dalison, B. & Wing, J.K. *Schizophrenia and Social Care*. Oxford University Press, London, 1966.

7. Creer, C. & Wing, J.K. *Schizophrenia at Home*. National Schizophrenia Fellowship, 1974.

8. Davies, F. *Passage Through Crisis*. Bobbs-Merrill, Indianapolis, 1963.

9. Miles, A. *The Mentally Ill in Contemporary Society*. Martin Robertson, London, 1981.

10. Laing, R.D. & Esterson, D. *Sanity, Madness and the Family*. Tavistock, London, 1964.

11. Bott, E. Family annd Crisis. In H. Freeman (Ed.) *Towards Community Mental Health*. Tavistock, London, 1971.

12. Williams, P. 'Psychiatric Disorder in the Community and in Primary Care'. Chapter 1, this volume.

13. Clausen, J. & Huffine, C. 'Sociocultural and Social – Psychological Factors Affecting Social Responses to Mental Disorders' *Journal of Health and Social Behaviour*. 16, 1975, 405.

14. Horwitz, A. 'Family, Kin and Friend Networks in Psychiatric Help-seeking' *Social Science and Medicine*. 12, 1978, 297-304.

15. Chester, P. *Women and Madness*. Doubleday, New York, 1972.

16. Rowbottom, R. & Hay, A. *Organisation of Services for the Mentally Ill*. Bioss, 1978.

17. *Better Services for the Mentally Ill*. HMSO, 1975.

18. Gay, P. & Pitkeathly, J. *The Community Care of the Discharged Hospital Patient*. Oxford Regional Health Authority and the Kings Fund, 1977.

19. Bean, P. 'Psychiatrists' Assessments of Mental Illness: a comparison of some aspects of Thomas Scheff's approach to labelling theory' *The British Journal of Psychiatry.* 135, 1979, 122-8.

20. Skuse. D.H. 'Attitudes to the Psychiatric Out-patients Clinic' *British Medical Journal.* 3, 1975, 469-471.

21. Wing, J.K. (Ed.) *Schizophrenia from Within.* National Schizophrenia Fellowship, London, 1975.

22. Watts, S. 'Social Work in Rural and Urban Areas: A Practice View' *Research Highlights.* 9, Department of Social Work, University of Aberdeen, 1985.

23. Grad, J. & Sainsbury, P. 'The Effects that Patients have on their Families' *British Journal of Psychiatry.* 114, 1968.

24. Brown, G.W., Sklair, F., Harris, T.O. & Birley, J.L.T. 'Life Events and Psychiatric Disorders, Part II: Nature of the Causal Link' *Psychological Medicine.* 3, 1973, 159-76.

25. Adler, L. 'Patients of a State Mental Hospital: the outcome of their hospitalization' In Rose, A. (Ed.) *Mental Health and Mental Disorder.* W. Norton, New York, 1955.

26. Evans, A., Bullard, D. & Solomon, M. 'The Family as a Potential Resource in the Rehabilitation of the Chronic Schizophrenic Patient: a study of 60 patients and their families' *American Journal of Psychiatry.* 117, 1961, 1075-83.

27. Holmes, T.H. & Rahe, R.H. 'The Social Readjustment Rating Scale' *Journal of Psychosomatic Research.* 11, 1967, 213-18.

28. Paykel, E.S. 'Recent Life Events and Clinical Depression'. In Gunderson, E.K.E. & Rahe, R.D. (Eds.) *Life Stress and Illness.* Charles Thomas, Illinois, 1974.

29. Ebringer, L. & Christie-Brown, J.R.W. 'Social Deprivation Amongst Short-Stay Psychiatric Patients' *British Journal of Psychiatry.* 136, 1980, 46-52.

30. Goldberg, E.M. & Morrison, S.L. 'Schizophrenia and Social Class' *Journal of Psychiatry.* 109, 1963, 785-802.

31. Rutter, M. & Madge, N. *Cycles of Disadvantage.* Heinemann, London, 1976.

32. Cooper, S.F., Leach, C., Storer, D. & Tonge, W.L. 'The Children of Psychiatric Patients: Clinical Findings' *British Journal of Psychiatry.* 131, 1977, 514-22.

33. McKnew, D.H., Cytryn, L., Efron, A.M., Gershon, E.S. & Bunney, W.G. 'Offspring of Patients with Affective Disorders' *British Journal of Psychiatry.* 134, 1979, 148-52.

34. Weissman, M.M., Paykel, E.S. & Klerman, G.L. 'The Depressed Woman as a Mother' *Social Psychiatry.* 7, 1972, 98-108.

35. Rice, E.P., Ekdahl, M.C. & Miller, L. *Children of Mentally Ill Parents.* Behaviour Publications, New York, 1971.

36. Newman, N. *The Children of Schizophrenics.* Unpublished Thesis, University of Oxford, 1970.

37. Garmezy, N. 'Children at Risk: The Search for the Antecedents of Schizophrenia Part II: Ongoing research Programs, Issues and Intervention' *Schizophrenia Bulletin.* 9, 1974, 55-125.

38. Brown, G.W., Birley, J.L.T. & Wing, J.K. 'Influence of Family Life on the Course of Schizophrenic disorders, a replication' *British Journal of Psychiatry.* 121, 1972, 241-58.

39. Leff, J. & Vaughan, C. 'The Interaction of Life Events and Relatives. Expressed Emotion in Schizophrenia and Depressive Neurosis' *British Journal of Psychiatry*. 136, 1980, 146-153.

40. Cartwright, A. & O'Brien, M. 'Social Class Variations in Health Care and in the Nature of General Practitioners' Consultations'. In Stacey, M. (Ed.) *The Sociology of the N.H.S.* Sociological Review Monograph no.22, University of Keele, 1976.

41. Meacher, M. *Scrounging on the Welfare*. Arrow, London, 1971.

42. Hill, J.M. The Psychological Impact of Unemployment *New Society*. 19th January 1978.

43. Brown, G. & Harris, T. *The Social Origins of Depression*. Tavistock, London, 1978.

44. Wing, J.K. Housing Environments and Mental Health. In Parry, H.B. (Ed.) *Population and its Problems*. Oxford University Press, Oxford, 1974.

45. Richman, N. Behaviour Problems in Pre-school Children: Family and Social Factors *British Journal of Psychiatry*. 131, 1977, 523-7.

46. Hudson, B. *Social Work with Psychiatric Patients*. Macmillan, London, 1982.

47. Olson, R. (Ed.) *Social Work and Mental Health*. Tavistock, London, 1984.

48. Leff, J.P. 'Family and Social Influences in Schizophrenia' *S.K. and F. Services to Psychiatry*. Vol.1, no.6, 1982, Smith, Kline and French Laboratories Ltd., Welwyn Garden City.

49. *The Friendship Club*. A social club for those in the community who are isolated and lonely, who may have had some contact with the psychiatric services. Aimed at an age group of 35+, it offers a wide programme of activities. Set up jointly by a social worker and a psychiatric nurse four years ago, it now has MSC funded workers though it is the members' committee that runs the club.

50. *Stepping Stones (Aberdeen)*. Initially started by a social worker six years ago for those in the 18-35 age group who were needing a 'stepping stone' between psychiatric hospital and the community. Since then it has extended its welcome to anyone who needs the social contact it can offer. The Club's main emphasis is on self − help and support.

51. *Pillar Contact*. This has evolved from the increasing awareness of members of the above two clubs that there was a need for a drop-in contact through the week and at weekends. It has a coffee-shop atmosphere and a loosely structured format providing a shop-front for other activities, clubs and organisations in the community. It is run by members of the clubs and has MSC funded workers. Although, at present, it opens for two sessions a week it is hoped to expand it in the future.

Psychiatric Crises in the Community: Collaboration and the 1983 Mental Health Act

T. Booth, C. Melotte, D. Phillips, J. Pritlove, A. Barritt and R. Lightup

INTRODUCTION

Recent trends in the management of psychiatric crises in the community are the result of two developments. The first is the growth of new kinds of crisis service, such as crisis centres and crisis teams, based on the theories of crisis intervention and social psychiatry [1]. The second is the disillusionment with the therapeutic optimism of the 1960s as manifested in pressures to reduce the power of professionals, especially doctors, and to increase the civil liberties of patients.

The new crisis resources springing up throughout the country represent a radical attempt to get away from the constraints of traditional, hospital-centred services. The essential elements of this alternative approach are close, inter-professional collaboration and teamwork; a focus on work in the community rather than in hospital; and an emphasis on the delivery of immediate, flexible and intensive help. Crisis resources may be based in either mobile teams or centres [2,3].

Concern about the civil liberties of people in psychiatric crisis gave rise to a number of critical studies of the working of the mental health legislation and was one of the main reasons for the passing of the 1983 Mental Health Act [4,5] for England and Wales and the Mental Health (Scotland) Act 1984. In particular, widespread disquiet arose over the use of the 1959 Mental Health Act's emergency procedure (Section 29) as the normal way of effecting a compulsory admission to psychiatric hospital [6]. The 1983 Act seeks to deal with this problem of crisis management by tightening up the legal and administrative loopholes over the use of emergency admissions [7] and by emphasising the principle of the 'least restrictive alternative' as the basis for decisions about care and treatment.

These two trends — the spread of new crisis services and of concern about the rights of patients — come together in the general issue of collaboration between the professional workers involved in a psychiatric crisis. Crisis intervention theory stresses the importance of teamwork, and the philosophy of the 1983 Act is that all the services should work together to safeguard the patient's rights as well as provide effective help.

ISSUES OF INTER-PROFESSIONAL COLLABORATION

Interdependence makes collaboration necessary between organisations as surely as between individuals. In the case of the health and social services it comes about for a variety of reasons, among the more important of which are the inter-relationship of needs in the community, the complementary nature of their services, considerations of effectiveness and the pursuit of value for money [8]. Each side commands resources, services or skills which the other needs to function effectively and cannot obtain elsewhere. The basic motive for collaboration in this context is rational self-interest.

Broadly, three levels of collaboration may be identified [9]:

- Collaboration at the *strategic level* in the making of policy, the setting of priorities and the allocation of resources.

- Collaboration at the *operational level* involving either the sharing of services or their integration at the point of delivery.

- Collaboration at the *practitioner level* in the case setting aimed at meeting the needs of individual clients.

At each of these levels, collaboration embraces a range of relationships or strategies. For example, Lindblom [10] has distinguished the following common 'methods of adjustment':

Bargaining or negotiation — through which each party seeks to reach agreement on a mutually acceptable trade-off.

Persuasion — by which one side tries to convince the other to accept its own definition of the situation.

Compensation — in which one party offers to reimburse the costs (financial or otherwise) of the other's compliance.

Reciprocity — a process of give-and-take from which both sides gain.

Prescription — in which one side defers to the other's authority or professional judgement.

Manipulation – in which both sides try to out-manoeuvre each other.

This paper is primarily concerned with the issue of collaboration between practitioners – social workers, GPs and psychiatrists – in their transactions over individual clients. Generally, relationships between social work and medicine at this level are held to be characterised more by conflict and recrimination than by reciprocity and mutual accommodation. Research suggests, however, that the true picture is more involved. Bruce [11], for instance, in a study of inter-agency co-operation in socio-medical preventive work with preschool children, identifies three modes of collaboration representing different points on a continuum of working practices. These are labelled:

Nominal – where collaboration is more a matter of lip-service than practice.

Convenient – where collaboration is practised so long as it serves the interests of all the parties.

Committed – where collaboration is seen to bring its own rewards and is practised for its own sake.

According to Bruce, the mode of collaboration that emerged between social workers and doctors was influenced by a number of organisational and inter-personal factors including their perceptions of each other's role and status, their interpretation of professional independence and their feelings of security or insecurity in working together, the extent of personal contact and the degree of trust, their regard for each other's skills and professional integrity, the formality of their relationship and the flexibility of their approach.

Huntington [12] explores in more detail the differences between social work and general medical practice that inhibit collaboration. She finds that marked *cultural* differences of knowledge, learned values, standards, technology, technique, work orientation, language, identity and relational orientations exist and that these are grounded in the different *structural* characteristics of the two occupations, particularly their demographic composition, the type of clientele they serve, the incomes received by practitioners and the settings in which they work. These structural and cultural differences are so pervasive, Huntington says, as to create two 'distinct symbolic worlds' whose members are unable to communicate with each other through the mists of mutual incomprehension.

Huntington's focus is on the macro or occupational level of analysis rather than relationships between individual practitioners. She would not seek to deny that some doctors and social workers commit themselves successfully to co-operative ways of working. After all, the main aim of collaboration is to act together, not to think alike [13]. Indeed, effective collaboration does not imply that, for instance, the different professionals involved in a psychiatric crisis — social workers, GPs and psychiatrists — should always agree about everything. Rather it entails that they should be able to handle their different contributions and viewpoints in a common spirit after the model of the crisis intervention team [2]. Huntington's real point is that attempts to improve relationships between social workers and doctors that fail to address the structural and cultural obstacles to better understanding are likely to produce only 'nominal' modes of collaboration. One of the aims of this paper is to consider if the effects of the 1983 Mental Health Act support this hypothesis.

COLLABORATION AND THE ACT

The general issue of collaboration between the medical and social work services in mental health cases had been the subject of growing concern throughout the 1970s. Fisher et al [14] showed, in their study of mental health social work, that psychiatrists and general practitioners were dismayed by the lack of regular personal contact with known social workers; by the apparently low priority accorded to mental health work by social services managers; by what they saw as a lack of knowledge about mental illness among social workers; and by social workers' inclination to focus on patients' civil liberties rather than their treatment. For their part, social workers felt that GPs in particular failed to consult them, lacked experience of mental health work and, too often, were ignorant of the mental health legislation.

These prejudices frequently came to a head during assessments for compulsory admission to psychiatric hospital. Under the 1959 Mental Health Act, a patient could be admitted compulsorily for observation (Section 25) or for treatment (Section 26). Both sections required two medical recommendations (usually from the patient's GP and a psychiatrist) and had to be accompanied by an application signed by a mental welfare officer or nearest relative. This safeguard was relaxed in cases of emergency (Section 29) when one medical recommendation only (in practice usually that of the GP) was required.

It is easy to see how the mutually negative attitudes of doctors and social workers, described by Fisher et al, could precipitate a breakdown in collaboration in a psychiatric crisis. Moreover, this danger was exacerbated by other pressures. General practitioners, used to assuming clinical responsibility and jealous of their clinical freedom, were naturally reluctant to call in a second opinion to endorse their own assessments. Also, consultant psychiatrists were often hard to get hold of or unwilling to visit. In these circumstances, social workers could feel pressurised by the atmosphere of crisis, the attitude of the GP, and the difficulty of contacting a psychiatrist into agreeing to the use of Section 29 in cases that were not genuine emergencies. In this way, emergency admissions came to make up the majority of all compulsory admissions under the 1959 Act, only falling from 56.8 per cent of the total in 1970 to 49 per cent in 1981 in the face of a rising outcry against this abuse. The potential damage to patients was very great: 'the main criticism of emergency admission is that the patient may be deprived of the privilege of a psychiatric opinion before his admission to hospital, and the obvious risk (of) .... an over-hasty admission, after which the damage is done.' [15]

These issues were taken up in the 1978 Review of the Mental Health Act 1959 [6]. Section 29 had been 'invoked more frequently than originally envisaged'. There should be a move towards crisis intervention services. Mental welfare officers should be better trained. And the aim of assessment should be to offer the 'least restrictive conditions' for the patient's care and treatment.

The 1983 Mental Health Act which eventually emerged from the process of review sets out to deal with these problems in three ways. In the first place, it aims to enhance the role and competence of mental health social workers (now called Approved Social Workers) who are assigned a specific and independent duty in the procedure for admission (Section 13) and are required to be specially trained and experienced (Section 114). As interpreted in the training courses run by social services departments, under the guidance of CCETSW, these provisions are designed to deal with the criticisms of social workers' lack of expertise and the low status given to mental health work. In addition, by limiting the number of ASWs in each Department, it has been made more likely that doctors will get to know and trust them.

Secondly, the new emergency section (Section 4) tightens up the procedures for emergency admission by reducing time periods and requiring details of the 'undesirable delay' that would result from having to seek a second medical opinion. Section 4 is now only to be used 'in exceptional cases' [16].

Thirdly, the 1983 Act embodies the philosophy of the 'least restrictive' alternative and carries with it the implication that services other than hospital admission, such as crisis centres, should be available for those who would benefit from them. In this context, the Mental Health (Scotland) Act 1984 carried into Scottish law the same concerns as the 1983 Act in England and

Wales. However, the differences north and south of the Border remain very considerable. In Scotland, the role of the Sheriff in authorising applications for compulsory admission alters the significance of the role of the Mental Health Officer (the Scottish equivalent of the Approved Social Worker) in the procedure. Most importantly, emergency admissions can be made simply on the basis of a medical recommendation, although the doctor is encouraged to obtain the consent of a Mental Health Officer (Section 24). Clearly, this procedure means that inter-professional collaboration in mental health crises in Scotland will have a flavour very different to that in England and Wales.

How far, then, have these reforms begun to relieve the problems of collaboration rooted in the nature of inter-professional relations and the working of the 1959 Act?

THE JUSSR STUDY OF PSYCHIATRIC CRISES

This paper draws on the findings of a survey of psychiatric crises in the community undertaken by the Joint Unit for Social Services Research (JUSSR) at Sheffield University. The survey was one of the first to investigate how the 1983 Mental Health Act is working in practice, and was undertaken in the metropolitan districts of Kirklees, Leeds and Trafford and the county of West Sussex. The survey was designed with three broad aims in mind:

- To identify the number and characteristics of psychiatric crises in the community requiring urgent assessment by social services staff.

- To identify resources used in working with these crisis cases, and also resources required but not available; in particular, in cases where hospital admissions take place, to discover whether the crises could have been coped with equally or more effectively if other resources had been available.

- To monitor the crisis-related work of the departments under the 1983 Mental Health Act, with particular reference to problems of collaboration and the handling of cases.

Information was gathered by asking social workers in each of the four authorities to complete a questionnaire every time they dealt with a psychiatric crisis. For the purpose of the study a crisis was defined as any event involving serious emotional or mental distress, or behaviour showing signs of a mental disorder, that requires urgent assessment by social services staff and a decision about whether an emergency exists which necessitates immediate action. The data on which this paper draws span a survey period of three to four months.

Before moving on to discuss the findings, a few qualifications about the survey method should be noted:

> *Consistency* – the definition of a crisis provided for the guidance of social workers was aimed at ensuring a high level of consistency between them in the classification of cases, but it does not remove the possibility of some variations occurring in its interpretation in individual cases.

> *Time Lags* – assiduous efforts were made to see that all questionnaires were completed within a fortnight of the crisis date but difficulties in monitoring the flow of work and following up individual social workers (especially members of Emergency Duty Teams) sometimes made this impossible and resulted in unsatisfactory delays.

> *Angle of Vision* – the study focussed on the crisis-related work of social services departments and provides only the social workers' perspective and judgements on the handling of the crises. Also, the emphasis is on the problems rather than the successes of collaboration.

> *Coverage* – close contact was maintained with social work teams in the four authorities, and regular reminders about the survey were issued in an attempt to ensure that questionnaires were completed and returned about all known crises, but it seems likely that some cases will have slipped through the net. Nevertheless, we are confident that, in each authority, all referrals and assessments for compulsory admission under the 1983 Act during the period of the survey were picked up.

CHARACTERISTICS OF THE CRISES AND THE RESPONSE

Altogether 202 crises were reported by social workers in the four authorities during the survey period. Over two-thirds of the referrals were women. There was a wide spread of ages, ranging from ll per cent of cases among 16-25 year olds to 7 per cent among people aged 75 or more. The largest single ten-year age band was the 26-35 year olds with 23 per cent of the cases. Over one-third of clients were living alone at the time of the crisis and a similar proportion were living with other adults. There was little variation between the authorities in the age and domestic circumstances of clients.

Nearly two-thirds of the reported crises occurred in clients' own homes. Over half (55 per cent) of all referrals came from doctors and 20 per cent from the police, with wide variations between authorities in the main sources of referral, presumably reflecting different administrative arrangements and patterns of working. Significantly, over a third of all cases (37.4 per cent) occurred outside normal office hours. These cases are particularly vulnerable to problems of collaboration simply because they are frequently dealt with by deputising doctors, duty psychiatrists, police surgeons or Emergency Duty Teams (EDTs) who, in many instances, will not know each other or the client.

In three-quarters of the cases, the client was known by the social worker to have a psychiatric diagnosis. Of these, almost 40 per cent were schizophrenic; a third suffered from depression or manic-depressive psychosis; senile dementia and personality disorders accounted for 7 per cent; and 10 per cent suffered from hypermania or mania. There were big differences between the authorities in the distribution of diagnoses. These may be due to random factors, disparities in local referral patterns, or variations in diagnostic criteria among psychiatrists.

Nearly three-fifths (59 per cent) of the 202 reported crises resulted in admission to a psychiatric hospital. Eighty-three clients (41 per cent of all cases) were admitted compulsorily, of whom a third (27 cases) were emergency admissions under Section 4. Thus 13 per cent of all reported crises led to an emergency compulsory admission. Table 1 compares the proportions of compulsory admissions by section in the survey under the new Act with the 1981 figures for England under the old Act.

TABLE 1

*Comparison of compulsory admissions by section
before and after the 1983 Mental Health Act*

Compulsory Admissions to hospital for		England* 1981%		JUSSR Survey 1984%
Assessment	Section 25	40.6	Section 2	58.5
Treatment	Section 26	10.4	Section 3	8.5
Emergency	Section 29	49.0	Section 4	32.9

*Source: DHSS, Inpatient Statistics: Mental Health Enquiry for England, 1981.

Clearly, there has been a substantial drop in the proportion of emergency applications, in favour of admissions for assessment, since the passing of the 1983 Mental Health Act. To this extent, there has been a shift in the direction intended by its sponsors. However, the Memorandum to the Act [16] makes it plain that Section 4 is only to be used in 'exceptional cases'. It would be difficult to argue that one-third of all compulsory admissions are in some way exceptional. The next section looks at how far this worryingly high rate of emergency admissions is related to continuing problems of collaboration between practitioners in the case setting such as are generally held to have been one of the reasons for the abuse of Section 29 of the 1959 Act.

This issue, however, must be seen in the context of available resources. One-fifth of all hospital admissions were felt, by social workers, to have been avoidable given a reasonable level of provision of alternative services. Furthermore, in over half (104) of all cases, social workers reported that many necessary services were unavailable at the time of the crisis. It was not possible to get in touch with a psychiatrist when needed in over a quarter of cases, and in a fifth the GP could not be contacted. A lack of social services resources was reported in 30 per cent of these cases, and in 14 per cent the duty social worker was unable to contact the client's regular caseworker. Again, in a third of these cases, a shortage of support in the community was mentioned: either from statutory services, such as community psychiatric nurses, or from informal sources, such as family, relatives or friends. Several reportedly necessary services were simultaneously unavailable in many cases. It is understandable, therefore, why social workers identified an unmet need in over a third of cases for a crisis intervention team or crisis resource centre.

Reference has been made already to the importance of developing crisis intervention services for the management of psychiatric crises in line with the philosophy behind the 1983 Act. The lack of crisis teams and crisis centres was said to be an important factor in the majority of reportedly avoidable admissions. In fact, the evidence of this survey may under-estimate their importance. It seems likely that the figures on avoidable admissions err on the low side in view of the lack of experience that many of the social workers in the study had had of practical alternatives to hospital. For instance, none of the four authorities had either a crisis team or a crisis centre in operation at the time of the survey.

COLLABORATION AND THE HANDLING OF THE CRISES

Problems of collaboration, varying in seriousness, were reported in 65 (32 per cent) of the 202 cases. They fell into three broad categories: problems of access; problems of attitudes or relationships; and problems of procedure.

Problems of Access

Problems of access arose most often because of difficulties in co-ordinating services or simply because of the unavailability of key people when the crisis erupted. In many instances they were unavoidable: the unfortunate result of busy schedules and the fact that psychiatric crises do not always occur at convenient times, as the following excerpts from the case reports show.

Case A   The client was extremely deluded, walking down the middle of the road believing himself to be indestructible. When questioned by police he became violent. A consultant psychiatrist was not available from 2.40 am until 8 pm and this delayed admission into hospital. The client had been taken by the police to the police station early in the morning. He was very disturbed and felt to be in need of hospital care. He was seen by a police surgeon, who signed a medical recommendation, and by a member of the Emergency Duty Team who wanted a second medical opinion, which was not available. I interviewed the client but was unable to obtain a visit from a psychiatrist until later that evening. I feel this client should have been admitted to hospital much earlier than he was, and that he should not have spent so many hours in a police cell, which could only have produced adverse effects.

Case B   The patient has a long psychiatric history and was last admitted 25 years ago. Since then she has been maintained on drugs by her GP. She recently moved to sheltered accommodation and began to display paranoid behaviour: not taking medication, feeding properly or washing herself. Deluded and verbally aggressive. Wandering at night. It took five hours from the initial visit by the social worker to admission to hospital in view of the time spent trying to contact GP and consultant psychiatrist to arrange joint visit, hospital bed and ambulance. The time wasted waiting for other services aggravated the crisis.

Such hitches and delays when the nature of the crisis calls for swift and immediate action are frustrating and potentially harmful but probably inevitable now and again: GPs may be off duty or unable to leave a clinic; other commitments may prevent the consultant psychiatrist making a domiciliary visit when the call comes through; the ambulance might not be able to get there straightaway. But problems of access encompass more than just these sorts of contingencies. They are also generated or exacerbated by working routines, professional methods and personal idiosyncracies of manner, style and approach.

Case C   Several reports of client wandering in confused state at night. At risk of accident and injury. Need for assessment. Psychogeriatrician saw patient and offered bed for next day but left matter with duty psychiatrist as she was going on leave. Patient would not accept voluntary admission. Duty consultant approached but would only accept patient on a Section 4 and before 5 pm. He would not himself come out that day, and insisted the case was an emergency. The 5 pm deadline did not leave enough time to get an approved doctor. In the interests of the client's safety a Section 4 admission was completed though ideally a Section 2 would have been more satisfactory.

Case D   Referral from GP requesting that an elderly lady be compulsorily admitted to hospital following a joint visit with a consultant psychiatrist earlier in the day. Since the death of her son two years ago she had become depressed and was not looking after herself properly. There were major problems in contacting the psychiatrist who had left no phone number or time when he would return to his office. He expected us to admit her for assessment under Section 2 although he had told the GP he would not be available to sign the forms until after her admission. This lady was seen in the afternoon yet was only referred to us as an emergency at 5 pm. Both the GP and the psychiatrist said she was at risk and would not agree to voluntary admission, yet in both instances we found no real problem. It is questionable whether this case should have come under the Mental Health Act. Are medical practitioners too quick to diagnose and then drop the crisis in the laps of social services?

Problems of Relationships

At this point, problems of access begin to shade into problems of relationships that disclose the kind of misunderstandings, frictions and conflicts anticipated in Huntington's 'two cultures' thesis. Generally, they appear to arise where there are differences between the social worker and doctor in their perceptions of each other's role and responsibilities, in their interpretations of the nature and gravity of the crisis, or in their views about what should be done. The following extracts from the case reports illustrate the sort of problems that occur:

Case E

The patient was suffering from severe congestive heart failure and refusing hospitalisation though treatment was necessary to save his life. A Consultant Psychiatrist had visited the previous day and diagnosed paranoid schizophrenia. The referral came through as a request for completion of a Section 2. On my first visit, I was unable to gain admission to the house to interview the patient. Following this abortive visit I saw the patient's GP who was very abusive and seemingly not willing to recognise the social worker's role. It was a complete balls-up by the GP and I was very unhappy about it.

Case F

The referral came at 5 pm and therefore could not be allocated to the area team. The night duty team did not feel confident about undertaking a section because of inexperience and I was called out to undertake the admission. This crisis was completely avoidable. The patient had been discharged from hospital in a psychotic state two weeks previously because of the ineptitude of the GP. He had felt the patient was 'not too mentally ill' and had refused to complete a section at that stage. He was unsure about the legal procedures for compulsory admission and claimed wrongly that the family were opposed to the admission.

Case G

The client had been undergoing a hypermanic episode: overactive, over-talkative, elated. She had caused a disturbance in a supermarket. She was admitted to the general hospital and placed on an open ward. She was refusing medication and demanding to leave, and will be allowed to do so if she makes a formal request to the staff. The GP refused to attend initially. After much pressure he agreed to do so. He was 'ignorant' of the law – felt Section 5 had to expire before he could execute a Section 3 – and refused to sign the section form on the grounds that the client was 'not bad enough'. I was unable to obtain an alternative doctor because it was holiday week. All in all, the crisis was handled very poorly, primarily because of the GP's attitude. He was unsure of his role and the legislation. He said he was under pressure to sign the form and also alleged the family were against the compulsory admission which they were not. This patient is likely to be discharged home in a psychotic state to the distress of her family and a danger to herself.

Interestingly, difficulties such as these were mostly a feature of relationships between social workers and the GPs. There was little evidence of similar problems between social workers and psychiatrists. Three reasons seem to emerge from the case reports. First, in the opinion of social workers, some GPs are reluctant to get involved in psychiatric cases and slow to respond to urgent referrals. This impression seems to be conveyed partly because many GPs are distrustful of social workers and cautious or wary about accepting their definition of a crisis. Partly, too, it is a consequence of the realities of their working day and the fact that GPs are not organised to provide an emergency service. Second, specialist mental health social workers usually have more experience of dealing with psychiatric crises than the average GP and are generally more familiar with the legal procedures and their implications. For doctors who are jealous of their clinical autonomy, having a social worker demur about what should be done for one of their patients can be hard to accept quietly. Third, where this relationship is further complicated by feelings of professional insecurity on the part of the doctor or hostility towards social workers it can easily lead to truculence and awkwardness. In short, some GPs find the role of the social worker under the mental health legislation an affront to their own professional status.

Problems of Procedure

However, not all the problems of relationships that impaired collaboration were of an inter-personal nature only. Many were precipitated or compounded by breakdowns in liaison or communication at an organisational level:

Case H   The client was discharged from the infirmary earlier in the day and 'dumped' on our car park, apparently having assaulted a nurse. He was complaining of paralysis of the left arm and leg. The infirmary did not want to know but the man was totally unable to cope at his flat. This was clearly a medical/psychiatric crisis. I phoned an ambulance and he was taken to the infirmary and then transferred to psychiatric hospital. In my view this should have happened hours earlier.

Examples such as this raise questions about the adequacy of operational links in the field that are beyond the scope of this paper. Generally, though, failures of operational co-ordination manifest themselves in the case setting as problems of procedure. For both are usually rooted in the administrative division of functions, powers and responsibilities between the health and social services [8].

The most common problems of procedure arose as a result of disagreements or uncertainties about clinical responsibilities and the interpretation of the Mental Health Act. Other causes were the unfamiliarity of many GPs with the legislation, and misjudgements on the part of deputising and duty staff, and others not practised in psychiatric work such as casualty doctors and police doctors.

Case I — This patient had been admitted to hospital voluntarily by a community psychiatric nurse and was now unwilling to stay though very confused and too difficult for his wife to contain. He had wandered off heading for home. The crisis was caused because a voluntary admission was made instead of the planned compulsory admission. Much out of hours work was made necessary for the consultant and the social worker because of the well-intentioned voluntary admission.

Case J — The client had been arrested after causing a disturbance in a church car park. She was unable to hold a rational conversation and related everything to God or the devil. The police doctor was not approved under Section 12 and was not familiar with the 1983 Act. He was offended when I suggested we contact the duty psychiatrist. Had the relatives not appeared and made it known they did not wish Mrs. M. to be admitted to hospital there could have been difficulties. Although the doctor was undecided about whether to section Mrs. M. he objected to another doctor being called.

Case K — The patient was most disturbed and had tried to throw herself through the window. A GP had been contacted who did not know the patient, nor was he qualified under Section 12 of the Act. He in fact completed a medical recommendation but this was not accepted by the social worker who called in the patient's GP.

Problems and Outcomes

The cases which presented the most serious difficulties of collaboration were, of course, those where all three types of problem – access, relationships and procedures – occurred together, as in the following example:

Case L   This was the third major episode of illness since the client's mother died in 1976. The police were called after he had caused an affray and some damage and he was taken to the police station where he was seen by a police surgeon and admitted informally to the psychiatric hospital. He walked out three times during the next three days, being returned twice by the police. On the third occasion, after he had been seen by his GP at home, I was asked to assess him with a view to compulsory admission. The GP, who'd had a disagreement with a colleague two years before during the client's last episode of illness, thought I should rubber-stamp the medical recommendations. When I did not do so he was more inclined to complain about me than work with me to help the client. I had difficulty discovering which consultant psychiatrist was responsible for the client and, at a crucial point, I could not get anyone to do a domiciliary visit. At one point it appeared that the GP and psychiatrist – having decided the client would have to be treated in hospital on an order – were denying access to any other form of treatment (e.g. medication under supervision at home or informal admission). At the time I felt that in declining to apply for compulsory admission but opting instead for assessment over a period of time I was taking on a great deal of responsibility. In the end, the psychiatrist did agree that the client could be admitted informally. Thereafter the attitude of the hospital staff to me was good but I had to initiate all communication and despite three specific requests the hospital failed to notify me of the client's discharge. A week later he committed suicide.

It had been suspected that cases involving compulsory admission might yield more problems of collaboration than others but analysis of the data showed no correlation between the incidence of reported difficulties and the type of outcome. Among compulsory admissions, problems were reported in just over a third of all Section 2 assessment cases (17 out of 48), a quarter of Section 4 emergency cases (seven out of 27), and three of the seven Section 3 treatment cases.

Interestingly, shortcomings in collaboration between practitioners did not invariably lead to dissatisfaction with the handling of the case on the part of social workers. Of the 202 cases for which information was available, 165 (82 per cent) were reported to have been dealt with satisfactorily in the circumstances and only 36 (18 per cent) were felt to have been mismanaged. In fact, no reservations were expressed about the response to the crisis in over half (35) of the 65 cases in which collaboration was seen to have been a problem, though most of those said to have been handled badly were ones in which collaboration had surfaced as an issue of concern (30 out of 36). Although the evidence is only tentative it seems that problems of relationships are more likely to lead to feelings of dissatisfaction with the handling of the case than problems of access or procedures. Certainly, there is a distinction between problems that only cause inconvenience and frustration for the practitioners themselves and those that rebound to the detriment of clients and their families.

Overall, the incidence of serious problems of collaboration was much lower than Huntington's analysis would lead one to expect, although, in Bruce's terms, the mode of collaboration rarely developed beyond a relationship of convenience. For the most part, the conclusion would seem to be that doctors and social workers have learned to live with their differences in dealing with psychiatric crises.

CONCLUSIONS

Two crucial pieces of evidence suggesting that the 1983 Mental Health Act is not working as fully as intended have been presented. Although the proportion of emergency admissions to hospital certainly appears to have fallen under the new procedure, the rate is still higher than would be expected if it was being used only in 'exceptional cases'. At the same time, the Act is also failing to prevent the compulsory admission of many patients who, in the assessment of social workers, could have been treated in less restrictive conditions. Both these findings imply that the Act has not succeeded, by itself, in safeguarding the rights of mentally ill people in the way those who led the campaign for a reform in the law envisaged.

Moreover, it has been shown that these disturbing signs of the continuing misuse of powers of detention cannot all be explained in terms of problems of collaboration at the practitioner level. This is no excuse for complacency on this front. Difficulties persist and the analysis above points to several ways in which relationships might be smoothed. For example:

- *Problems of access* might be eased through having more approved doctors, more specialist mental health social workers, better duty psychiatrist systems that ensured there always was a psychiatrist available and, importantly, consultant psychiatrists who served specific geographical areas — an innovation that would improve their liaison and relationships with GPs as well as social workers.

- *Problems of attitudes* might be lessened by closer working links between ASWs and psychiatrists (possibly through some form of crisis intervention service), by the joint training of, especially, EDT social workers, deputising doctors and police surgeons, and by better liaison in general between GPs and social workers through attachment schemes, joint training initiatives and Local Medical Committees.

- *Problems of procedure* might be minimised or prevented by a move towards community mental health teams or by the introduction of an arbitration procedure along the lines suggested by Fisher *et al.* [14].

Nevertheless, problems of collaboration were reported in only a minority of cases and even then they did not generally lead to dissatisfaction on the part of social workers with the outcome of the crises.

The evidence of this survey suggests that the reasons why the 1983 Act has not prevented avoidable admissions to hospital or the excessive use of emergency sections are not to be found in the failure of practitioners to collaborate because of the differences in their backgrounds, as Huntington's hypothesis might lead one to suppose, but in obstacles at the operational and strategic levels of collaboration. Decisions that are against the best interests of patients and contrary to the spirit of the Act are being dictated by service constraints. It is lack of resources, poor co-ordination of existing services and inadequate planning, rather than inherent problems of inter-professional relationships, that are mainly implicated in the unsatisfactory handling of psychiatric crises in the community. These constraints on the development of adequate community services for mentally ill people, equipped to respond in a swift and co-ordinated fashion to psychiatric crises, are shown most clearly in the stunted growth of crisis intervention services. If the 1983 Act is to fulfil the principles that led to its passing then enough resources must be provided to meet the fundamental requirements of crisis intervention theory for immediate, flexible and intensive help.

References

1. Caplan, G. *An Approach to Community Mental Health*. Tavistock, London, 1979.

2. Bouras, N. & Tufnell, G. 'Mental Health Advice Centre: The Crisis Intervention Team'. Research Report No.2, Lewisham Multi-Professional Psychiatric Research Unit, Lewisham and North Southwark Health Authority, 1983.

3. Newton, S.M. 'Coventry Mental Health Crisis Intervention Project: Report on First Year 1983-84'. Social Services Department, Coventry, 1984.

4. Gostin, L. 'The Mental Health Act from 1959-75: Observations, Analyses and Proposals for Reform'. MIND, London, 1975.

5. Gostin, L. 'A Human Condition' *MIND*. London, 1977.

6. *Review of the Mental Health Act 1959*. Cmnd 7320, HMSO, London, 1978.

7. Gostin, L. 'A Practical Guide to Mental Health Law'. *MIND*, London, 1983.

8. Booth, T. 'Collaboration and the Social Division of Planning' *Collaboration and Conflict: Working with Others*. Research Highlights No.7, University of Aberdeen, 1983, 10-32.

9. Booth, T. 'Collaboration between the Health and Social Services' *Policy and Politics*. 9, 1, 1981, 23-49.

10. Lindblom, C.E. *The Intelligence of Democracy*. Free Press, New York, 1965.

11. Bruce, N. 'The Social Work/Medicine Interface'. Department of Social Administration, University of Edinburgh, September 1978.

12. Huntington, J. *Social Work and General Medical Practice*. Allen and Unwin, London, 1981.

13. Kahn, A.J. 'Institutional Constraints to Interprofessional Practice'. In Rehr, H. (Ed.) *Medicine and Social Work: an Exploration in Interprofessionalism*. Prodist, New York, 1974.

14. Fisher, M., Newton, C. & Sainsbury, E. *Mental Health Social Work Observed*. Allen and Unwin, London, 1983.

15. Hoggett, B. *Mental Health Law*. Sweet and Maxwell, London, 1984.

16. *Mental Health Act 1983*: Memorandum on Parts I-VI, VIII and X. DHSS, London, 1983.

The authors are all members of the Joint Unit for Social Services Research at Sheffield University.

Mental Health Officers and the Scottish Acts of 1960 and 1984

Chris McGregor

INTRODUCTION

The Mental Health (Scotland) Act 1984 became operational on 30th September 1984, a year later than its English counterpart. As far as is known, there has not yet been any formal survey of its workings, comparable with that of the 1983 Act undertaken by the Joint Unit for Social Services Research at Sheffield University and described in this issue of Research Highlights. The following comments are based on personal observations and my research study on practice under the 1960 Act [1].

THE MENTAL HEALTH ACTS OF 1959 AND 1960

The roles of the Mental Health Officer in Scotland and Mental Welfare Officer (now Approved Social Worker) in England, have developed along different lines, reflecting the contextual differences of the two legal frameworks.

Traditionally the English officer played a key role in the transporting of the patient to hospital; the Scottish officer had a lesser role at this stage as the system had developed of Sheriff Officers and later the General Practitioner and ambulance service having responsibility for transportation. These different traditions were reflected in the emergency provisions of the 1959 and 1960 legislation. In the English 1959 Act, the MWO, or any relative, was charged with the responsibility of making the emergency application and obtaining medical support for it: in the Scottish 1960 Act, it was the other way round; one medical officer could make the emergency application, obtaining consent of any relative or MHO 'where practicable'.

In England, the MWO could and did play a crucial role in the admission of someone to hospital. He had powers to call for a psychiatric opinion and was responsible for documents and escorting. He could also use his discretion, to an extent, in deciding whether he judged appropriate an emergency order or an observation order. Although the power to be applicant was also given to a relative, it appears that most orders came to be signed by MWOs [2,3].

In Scotland the pattern emerged of the MHO having only a minimal role in effecting the emergency admission of a patient to psychiatric hospital. The emergency order was instigated by a medical person and over the years it became apparent that only a small proportion included MHO consent. One survey showed MHO involvement under the emergency terms of Section 31 in only six out of 190 admissions [4] and another study mentioned no MHO involvement in 100 consecutive emergency admissions [5].

In Scotland the main area of MHO activity under the 1960 Act was in relation to making the application for full formal compulsory detention under Section 24 when a nearest relative was unavailable, unable or unwilling to do so. This was akin to procedures under Sections 25 and 26 of the 1959 Act with the significant variation that in Scotland the Sheriff had to approve the application and the MHO had the right to decline to make the application if not satisfied about its appropriateness.

In the late 1970s it was apparent that MHO practice was peripheral to mainstream social work and the incidence and standards of practice were variable. John Tibbitt [6] conducted a Scottish Office Social Research Study in 1978, revealing much confusion about the MHO role among both management and workers. His sample revealed a very low incidence of MHO involvement in cases of compulsory admission as well as marked regional variation in appointments to MHO status, ranging from all employed social workers to seniors only. There was also little consensus about what the MHO should be doing. Outside the social work profession there was indifference to the MHO role. What seemed to be wanted was expeditious compliance with the medical and legal professions when willing relatives were not available to complete the paperwork. It seems fair to say that it is only within the past five years or so that the Scottish social work profession has begun to address its contribution to compulsory procedures and to set standards of practice.

MHO PRACTICE UNDER SECTION 24, 1960 ACT

A study was carried out in the Royal Edinburgh Hospital, examining the involvement of MHOs in all Section 24 procedures, from May 1981 to May 1982. It charted the involvement of 17 MHOs in 94 instances of proposed formal detention. The MHOs comprised 12 hospital based workers and five area team workers. They had all been designated under a Lothian policy introduced in 1981 and had been on an in-service training course.

Two studies of MHO work in England [3,7] found that a) MHOs were concerned about their lack of experience of compulsory admission work and their lack of opportunities for gaining expertise; b) bad working relationships between psychiatrists and social workers. My own experience of working as a MHO had been in marked contrast to that depicted by Bean, and the formulation of the aims of the study were strongly influenced by this direct practice experience and awareness of a working situation where there was concern to provide good professional standards. There were also, in my view, regular patterns of MHO involvement and examples of inter-professional co-operation. The main aims of this study were thus to:

1. ascertain and assess the tasks the MHOs actually undertook

2. clarify some of the needs of patients

3. identify sources of difficulties and dilemmas and make recommendations concerning future policy and practice.

It was shown that MHOs can and do make a significant professional contribution to the procedures required for the compulsory detention of patients. In particular, the importance of social assessment was demonstrated. Non-medical factors such as social circumstances prior to admission; family relationships and attitudes, patients' reactions to being compulsorily detained; the hospital as a setting; and resources available to support the patient, all had the potential for influencing the decision about the necessity for a Section 24 order and the MHO was seen to be the person who most consistently appraised and reported on these aspects. The medical and nursing professions' proper preoccupation with the patient's need for and right to treatment required balancing by such reporting on these and other relevant matters.

The MHO's interaction with nearest relatives was revealed as important, reflecting the need to make the relatives an integral part of the procedures at a level they could tolerate and which maximised possibilities for the patient, yet which upheld the spirit and terms of the Act. This study showed that MHOs were the one group who systematically drew the relatives into the process and worked with them as people in crisis with their own particular responses and needs, rather than simply using them as sources of information or as potential applicants for Section 24 orders.

After-care was identified as an area for development requiring more systematic attention from social work. The unmet needs of the patient group were marked and augured ill for their future. In many cases there appeared to be an ambiguous relationship with the hospital; enforced detention, however it was viewed, encouraged dependency; in-patiency was closely guarded but the return to the community could be remarkably unstructured. Sometimes the argument that the patient wanted to put the experience behind him seemed to be brought into play as an excuse for poor follow up. The idea of the hospital having a special responsibility towards patients who had been or were still subject to a compulsory detention order was not markedly evident in the course of this study. Yet the vulnerability of the patients was quite striking and called for after-care by support on both medical and social fronts, recognising that a major programme of rehabilitation and maintenance was required if breakdown and re-admission were not going to ensue.

It was clear that local authorities required to have policies about the MHO service which resulted in a regular flow of practice for individuals to maintain and develop skills. It is counter productive in terms of professional credibility and demonstrable expertise, to have an over-abundance of MHOs, most of whom get no opportunity to act. Training and interpretation of policy into professional social work terms were highlighted as crucial matters in relation to the calibre of MHO performance. In general terms it seemed that the role of the MHO had to be defined and described in a way which could be more widely accepted and more uniformly applied.

MHOs WORKING WITH THE 1984 ACT

What patterns of MHO practice are discernible in an appraisal of the first six months of working with the new Mental Health (Scotland) Act?

EMERGENCY PROCEDURES: SECTION 24

It is evident that hospital doctors and GPs are making efforts to get either family or MHO consent to Section 24 emergency detentions, in marked contrast to widespread non-observance of this under the 1960 Act. The 1984 requirement that a copy of all emergency certificates be sent to the Mental Welfare Commission has introduced a new note of accountability. There are still, however, a significant number of 'non-consents'. In my personal screening of three months' figures, it emerged that 'non-consents' constituted 22 per cent of all Sections 24 received. In the variety of explanations given for not obtaining consent, the facts that in 68 per cent there was no reference whatsoever to trying to contact an MHO and in only 8 per cent was there reference to having tried unsuccessfully to contact an MHO, are of relevance in the context of this paper. Does this denote ignorance or high-handedness on the part of doctors? Does it reflect inadequate systems of MHO cover or perhaps failure by social work departments to publicise arrangements? For whatever reasons there are certainly problems of collaboration.

MHOs are raising questions about the value of their consent if it is 'uninformed' in the sense that the patient is unknown, the time is short and alternatives unavailable. Some have been suggesting that it is better to withhold consent than give it uncertainly in response to a persuasive doctor. The spirit of the Act is that MHO's or relative's consent be obtained to ensure that a dimension other than medical is introduced. Emergency procedures are in essence crisis situations where all professionals have to work within the constraints of time and perhaps limited information. I am of the opinion that it would be unfortunate if there was to be any widespread development of MHOs not participating. It would be much better if the MHO could be enabled to practise with assurance and authority in emergency procedures. Clearly, adequate training would be needed to accomplish this.

Early figures indicate that relatives are giving consent in about twice as many instances as MHOs. What is not yet known is if MHOs are performing any enabling function in the process of relatives giving this consent.

SHORT TERM DETENTION ORDERS/SECTIONS 26

This short term procedure is an entirely new concept within Scottish Mental Health law as previously all detention beyond the seven day emergency provision had to be approved by a Sheriff. In these early stages of new practice, my impression is that a high proportion of these Sections 26 are happening with the consent of the nearest relative or the MHO, again with relatives' consent outnumbering MHO consent. Of interest is the question of what does the consent-obtaining process consist? Are doctors and/or relatives explaining the implications of the short term order and affording choice, or is it a much more implicit process? I suspect there is wide variation of practice.

SOCIAL CIRCUMSTANCE OR MHO REPORTS

As in England, the requirement to report on the social circumstances of any person subject to compulsory detention beyond an emergency period, has been introduced. Some discussion is taking place about whether these reports should become known as 'Social Circumstance' or 'MHO' Reports. In Scotland the MHO has responsibility for providing the report under Section 26(5) and not any social worker as under the 1983 Act. Also the Scottish report is provided for the Responsible Medical Officer and the Mental Welfare Commission. In 1960, Scotland chose to retain the former Board of Control under the new title of Mental Welfare Commission so over the years has had the benefit of a body charged with an overall protective function in respect of mentally handicapped and mentally ill people.

As Social Work Officer of the Mental Welfare Commission I see all of these reports and consider that the profession is providing them assiduously. At this time, guidelines of criteria and format have still not been issued by the Social Work Services Group and variation in style and content is evident and understandable. I tend to the view that MHOs should make more of their professional assessment of the patient's circumstances, with an appraisal of alternatives to detention, the risk factors and the formulation of a plan for the future. I believe we have a duty to draw attention to gaps in services and resources. It is, however, early days and the social work profession has every right to ask what use is being made of the reports and to monitor this aspect of practice carefully.

SECTION 18

Formal detention beyond 28 days still requires approval of the application by the Sheriff. In contrast with the position of consent-giving in Sections 24 and 26, MHOs predominate over relatives as applicants under Section 18. In the most recent 50 I have looked at, MHOs were applicant in 41 cases and nearest relatives applicant in nine. This is in line with my own findings in 1982 [1], where MHOs were applicant in 61.7 per cent of cases and nearest relatives in 38.3 per cent. Forty-two per cent of relatives actively chose not to be applicant, as opposed to being excluded by distance or being out of touch, and the majority did so because they wanted protection from the patient's reaction and wanted to maximise the chances of improving the relationship. This area of working with relatives continues to be, I believe, one of the main aspects of MHO practice.

There appears to be an increase in the number of Sheriff's hearings in relation to compulsory detention. Section 113 says 'In any appeal to the Sheriff under this Act, or in any proceedings relating to an application for admission to a hospital or for reception into guardianship, the Sheriff shall give the patient an opportunity to be heard......'. The Act goes on to say that only if the patient's health would be prejudiced should the opportunity to be heard be denied and then his representative should be heard. Sheriffs are offering hearings in many more cases and this has had the effect of bringing many more MHOs into such procedures. In Lothian, for example, there were 16 Sheriff hearings involving MHOs in the first three months of the new Act's life [8]. Training courses will be required to take account of this and local arrangements with Regional Solicitors' Departments will have to be set up, where these are not already in existence.

Under the 1984 Act the MHO no longer has the right to decline the application but may submit a recommendation of non-approval to the Sheriff, with his reasons for so doing. To date I have only encountered this happening once and the application was approved despite the MHO's views. Again this is an area of practice which requires careful monitoring.

CONCLUSION

At present there is little published on the subject of the MHO. Why this should be is a matter for conjecture but the piecemeal development of the MHO role and the ambiguous links with mainstream social work have probably meant that there has been no one group in a position to comment on issues and describe practice from a strong knowledge base. It is likely that the limited view of MHO duties held by other professions has also contributed to it being a relatively unheeded aspect of mental health legislation.

The requirements of the 1984 Act call for a professionally qualified MHO service as an integral part of compulsory detention procedures. The legislators have conferred a role of assessment and support, with local authorities' services to be available to patients and their families. It is not a particularly propitious time for social work to be extending its scope and enhancing its performance, and research can make an important contribution by fostering interest and by evaluating and commenting on the response of the profession.

References

1. McGregor, C.E. *'Mental Health Officers: A Study of Professional Practice Relating to Section 24 Admissions'*. MSc. Thesis, Stirling University, 1983.

2. Hoggett, B. *Mental Health*. Sweet and Maxwell, London, 1976, p.8.

3. Bean, P. *Compulsory Admissions to Mental Hospitals.* John Wiley & Sons, 1980.

4. McGregor, C.E. 'Survey of Section 31 Orders in Royal Edinburgh Hospital: Period 1.10.80 to 30.9.81, unpublished.

5. Chiswick, D. 'Patterns of Use and Attitudes towards Mental Health (Scotland) Act 1960'. M.Phil. Thesis, Edinburgh, 1978.

6. Tibbitt, J. *Social Workers as Mental Health Officers.* HMSO, 1978.

7. Danbury, H. 'Mental Health Compulsory Admissions – The Social Worker's Viewpoint' *Social Work Today.* 7, 6, 10.6.76.

8. McGregor, C.E. 'Crossing a Mental Health Border' *Social Work Today.* 16, 30, 1.4.84.

Anxious? Worried? Upset? The Role of a Mental Health Advice Centre

Jan McLaren and Arnold Bursill

INTRODUCTION

Estimates of the prevalence of psychiatric morbidity vary widely according to the criteria used. What is certain, however, is that a large proportion of the adult population, perhaps as much as a quarter, suffers from some degree of emotional disorder during any one year [1]. Although most of these people seek help from general practitioners, about one in 12 does not and, of those who do, a third are not treated and indeed may not need medical treatment. Our concern in this paper, and in the work of the Centre described later, is with this unmet need. We argue that there is a gap in the provision of care between informal support in the community and treatment within the medical services. We describe an experiment designed to provide help for the 10 per cent of the population who fall between those two modes of care.

RESPONSES TO STRESS

It is not clear at what point to draw the line between accentuated normal states and psychiatric morbidity. The experience of stress-related symptoms is part of normal expectation of living. Subjective reactions to significant life events, to positive and negative changes in environment, occupation, status and relationships will normally span a wide spectrum of feeling states.

Some individuals have the inner resources to cope with most of life's stresses, either at the behavioural (active problem solving) or at the cognitive (altered thoughts and attitudes) level. Many seek help from others.

Community Resources

Traditionally, many of the symptoms defined by Goldberg and Huxley [1] as indicators of psychiatric morbidity — anxiety, depression, tension — have been relieved through support from culturally determined social networks. Relatives, friends, neighbours and, for some, ministers of religion or colleagues at work, have all been expected to share in coping with distress. Even the existence of just one intimate, confiding relationship, be it friend, lover or close member of the family, has been shown to ameliorate stress and obviate depression [2].

As a complement to these informal social supports a number of service agencies have been established, often instigated by voluntary lay bodies, to deal with the effects of specific life problems; the Samaritans and the Marriage Guidance Council are among the most widely available of these. The emergence of the self-help movement, organised by those with specific 'life problems' in common, has extended the range of lay support systems available [3].

A number of factors combine, however, to make these community resources inaccessible, inappropriate or inadequate for many people. Geographical and social class mobility have made rare the readily available extended family. Effective contraception has contributed to the smaller size of the 'nuclear family'. Living in conurbations has led to more people feeling alienated and anonymous. Increasing secularisation has removed from many the comfort and support derived from a religious faith and from the church.

Even where informal social networks are available, many people are reluctant to communicate their personal fears and anxieties, or intimate details of their relationship problems, to people with whom they interact on a regular basis. It is difficult for those who depend on the successful functioning of others in particular roles to accept that they too may be vulnerable in other aspects of their lives. As a result of their own needs bias in the kind of support offered is unavoidable. Other associates may attempt to trivialise problems by offering bland reassurance but placation does nothing to help confront and tackle the issues causing distress. Many people need to have their disclosures treated confidentially; friends and relatives do not always respect such confidences. Often individuals feel that intimate details of their personal lives may be perceived as burdensome or an embarrassment to others, and, indeed, *they* may feel inhibited in discussing them with people they know well. Many may have difficulty in finding a friend with the time to explore fully the causes of their distress. Even sharing their 'problems of living' with others who have experienced a similar situation is not necessarily helpful; although it is reassuring to know that they are not alone in their suffering, successful methods of coping are not always generalisable. Those offering help and advice are often limited in the options they offer by their own idiosyncratic experience and reactions to the problem.

Professional Help

Many people turn to the professional carers for help with their emotional problems. With the increasing medicalisation of society many approach their general practitioner for support and advice. It is known, however, that on average, GPs spend rather less than ten minutes seeing any patient [4,5]. Extended counselling of patients is, therefore, rarely feasible, even when the GP considers such an option to be potentially therapeutic. The upshot of most such encounters, when it is not reassurance alone or referral to the psychiatric services, will be a prescription for a psychotropic drug. The efficacy of such chemotherapy is too rarely monitored. Often the dosage fails to be modified with changing drug sensitivity or increasing side effects, or to be stopped at the end of an appropriate course of treatment. Many courses of treatment should terminate after three to six months, yet large numbers of patients stay on such treatments for years, maybe decades [6,7]. These drugs may relieve the initial symptoms of stress but they do not of themselves confront or alleviate the causes. Further, it is questionable to what extent the medical practitioner should be expected to prescribe a solution to what may essentially constitute problems in living.

In response to these dilemmas – pressure on the GP's time and the possible inappropriateness of a medical response – there have been attempts to make counselling more readily available in primary care settings. Social workers, counsellors, psychologists and psychiatrists have worked alongside GPs in a variety of experiments. A few mental health centres have been instituted [8] [9] but their main objective has been to make *psychiatric* care more accessible. A rather different concept lay behind the development of the Oxford Isis Centre where the emphasis was less on providing conventional psychiatric diagnostic and treatment services in a community setting and more upon creating a flexible counselling service for a range of emotional problems which might normally be considered below the threshold of psychiatric morbidity [10]. In this sense it could be regarded as a preventive service. It is primarily a walk-in, self-referral centre similar in this respect to the mental health clinics which are becoming increasingly common in the U.S.A. [11]. It also shares a number of the characteristics of the innovation described later.

Social work interventions in this field, apart from the role of approved social workers or mental health officers in hospital admissions, have been of two main kinds. Firstly, social workers with special interests in mental health problems have been attached under various administrative arrangements to medical teams. Secondly, and more commonly, 'mental' problems form part of the generic social worker's case load. Five per cent of cases referred to Scottish social work departments were specifically concerned with mental illness and the proportion rises to 18 per cent if the definition of mental care widens to include, for example, alcohol problems [12]. Many potential clients, however, may perceive social work as being primarily about practical problems. Practical and emotional problems are often intertwined in rather complex ways, however, and social workers can do much to prevent such problems either being neglected or over-medicalised.

Non-Professional Interventions

Most of the experiments referred to above use professional resources, usually psychiatrists and/or psychologists. It is questionable, however, whether such specialised intervention is always necessary, and it is possible that befriending and sympathetic, non-directive counselling, carried out by trained lay volunteers, can provide an effective alternative. It must be emphasised that the emotional and stress-related problems in question are not, or have not yet become, unequivocal psychiatric disorders; for these, skilled professional treatment will still be required.

Research carried out mainly in the United States has suggested that the work of lay counsellors or professionals with a minimum of training may be as effective therapeutically as that carried out by therapists with years of training. The work of Truax and Carkhuff emphasised the triad of positive elements which they considered to be necessary for effective counselling and which were found to be common elements across divergent theories [13]. They were genuineness, nonpossessive warmth and empathy. This 'triad' seems to identify something close to a warm, loyal friendship. Indeed, according to this view, a deep theoretical approach is likely to obscure such positive ingredients in the relationship. Space does not allow a review of the evidence: it was deemed sufficiently strong to justify the use of lay counsellors developing with clients a relationship of friendship and support aimed at problem identification and problem-solving, far removed from in-depth psychodynamic psychotherapy. Relatively unsophisticated individuals, it is asserted, can greatly improve their therapeutic skills with limited hours of training providing that the 'triad' is focussed upon and the would-be counsellor is an 'inherently helpful person'. Evidence of this kind, together with a wish to provide a service for those who lack the inter-personal resources resources to cope effectively with their stress-related problems, lay behind the establishment of the Crown Street Mental Health Advice Centre.

THE CROWN STREET MENTAL HEALTH ADVICE CENTRE

Introduction

The Aberdeen and North East Association for Mental Health, a voluntary organisation founded in 1951, has as its main concern 'Mental Health within the Community both in respect of those who have had mental illness and in relation to the promotion of greater mental health among ordinary people' [14]. In pursuit of these aims the Association has a tradition of innovating a new service, proving it, and having successfully done so, seeking to have it taken over by the public sector. The first group home for former psychiatric patients in Aberdeen was established by the Association, for example. A part time Day Centre was founded in 1975 to provide a social and rehabilitative milieu for former psychiatric patients. The aim of the latter is to provide friendship and mutual self-help for people whose confidence, social skills and social contacts have been undermined as a result of mental illness.

During the late 1970's the Association and, in particular, a psychologist (Arnold Bursill), a Deputy Director of Social Work (Archie Robb) and a psychiatrist (Dr. Ronald Stewart), decided to address the gap in services identified by Goldberg and Huxley [1]. After protracted discussions the Association agreed to develop a Mental Health Advice Centre for members of the public suffering from emotional distress. The Centre would have the following characteristics: a) it would be located in the centre of Aberdeen accessible by public transport to all the residents of the city and the surrounding rural hinterland; b) the Centre would not provide medical or psychiatric treatment. Where such treatment was thought to be appropriate, it would be suggested that the client sought his GP's advice; c) the objective would be to provide information, and where necessary to listen, and support, the overall aim being to help the user help himself, and become stronger to do so in the future; d) the Centre would be readily accessible to the public, who would walk in without a prior appointment; e) users would be self-referred and would therefore have sought help voluntarily with problems *they* had defined as being of significance in their lives; f) the Centre would be flexible in the kind of service offered, responding where possible to the demands made upon it by users; g) the activities of the Centre would be co-ordinated by one paid full time Development Officer, assisted by a paid part time secretary and a team of lay volunteers; h) the form and style of operation of the Centre would reflect to a certain extent the interests and orientation of the co-ordinator, together with a Management Committee appointed to oversee the development of the Centre; i) as an overall objective, the Centre would seek a role complementary to those of existing community resources, and generally offering an alternative to other informal and formal support systems.

The Development of the Centre

The Association obtained funding from the Social Work Services Group (under Section 10 of the Social Work Act) to cover approximately three-quarters of the running costs for a three year experimental period. Supplementary funding was obtained from the Grampian Health Board and the Grampian Social Work Department, but a substantial residual amount remained to be raised by the Association. It was decided, partly for ideological reasons but also on economic grounds, to co-ordinate the activities of the existing part time Day Centre with the proposed Advice Centre. They would be combined administratively under one roof but would retain separate, complementary functions.

The Development Officer to co-ordinate both activities was selected in November 1982. It had been considered desirable that the person appointed should have some professional qualification and experience, without being too readily identifiable with a particular professional model of service provision. An eclectic background was believed to be conducive to the development of an innovative community based project. The person appointed, Jan McLaren, qualified in education and had spent the previous 11 years co-directing an epidemiological study of mental handicap at the Institute of Medical Sociology in Aberdeen. Starting in February 1983, she spent six months preparing for the opening of the Centre. A continuous task was the compilation of a directory of resources, local and national, identifying possible sources of help with specific problems so that users of the centre would be able to contact other, specialist agencies if they seemed more appropriate. Personal contact was made with a wide range of voluntary and statutory agencies, eliciting information about their provision and discussing the role to be played by the new centre.

The main task was to formulate a viable method of operation. The terms of reference still left a number of issues to be resolved. Among the most intractable was the style of operation. Opposing, somewhat conflictual, models were proposed. One concept entailed an anonymous, private, one-to-one relationship between counsellor and client. The other constituted a social drop-in centre, in which the 'client' joined an informal group of other users and volunteers all engaged in an open system of support. There was no question that there was a need in the community for both kinds of centre but limited resources of space, personnel and time, together with the personal preference of those involved, made it impractical to attempt to develop both simultaneously. The two conceptual models could not be reconciled within one organisation although elements from both were incorporated. The design which evolved was closer to that of an individual counselling service.

Short term, supportive counselling, emphasising in the training of counsellors their development of feelings of genuineness, warmth and empathy, was advocated for use in the Centre. Such counselling for emotional and stress-related problems was not known to be readily available elsewhere in Aberdeen. Counsellors were, also, to be encouraged to incorporate elements of client problem identification and solution finding in their work. These procedures, derived from a different psychological tradition, are applied usually for stress reduction and coping management, and have been empirically demonstrated to be efficacious [15].

The recruitment and selection of volunteers became a major priority. A training committee of a psychiatrist, psychologist and social worker collaborated with the Development Officer in planning an initial training programme for the first eight volunteers. Accommodation was found centrally. Exclusive use of three floors of a terraced house, owned by the Society of Friends, was leased to the Association. The building at 100 Crown Street appeared from the outside to be like an ordinary house, located within 200 yards of the city's main Post Office and easily accessible by public transport.

The Centre opened in August 1983 for three sessions each week, a morning, an afternoon and an evening. In September 1984, when sufficient experience had been gained and additional paid and volunteer staff recruited, the Advice Centre expanded to ten sessions each week, four mornings, four afternoons and two evenings. Meanwhile, the Day Centre expanded from two afternoon sessions each week to three in February 1984 and four in the following October. The Centre participated in initiating self-help groups for anorexics, depressives, bereaved parents and agoraphobics.

CHARACTERISTICS OF THE CROWN STREET MENTAL HEALTH ADVICE CENTRE

Staffing

The Centre has at present a Development Officer and a part time secretary. During the first year it became obvious that even with an increasing complement of volunteers, additional stipendiary staff were essential to maintain and expand the work. Accordingly, two part time receptionist/ counsellors, funded under an M.S.C. Community Programme, were taken on in July 1984 to provide the first point of contact for users of the centre. They provide continuity from day to day for clients and staff and help maintain the basic routine integral to the organisation. The Centre depends very heavily upon its volunteer lay counsellors. It was estimated that a minimum of two counsellors would be required to man each session in addition to the receptionist and the Development Officer, who counsels during some sessions. With the Centre open for ten sessions each week, therefore, a complement of at least 20 volunteers available for one session is required. At present the Centre has 24 trained volunteers with a further 12 undergoing training. Given the restricted space at Crown Street, with a maximum of four counselling rooms available, the optimum number of counsellors required is around 40 working once a week.

Counsellor Training

Four cohorts of volunteers have completed training. The 17 women and seven men currently working come from a range of backgrounds, with the majority possessing a professional qualification and experience. The professions most widely represented are education and psychology, with six volunteers from each; the remaining staff comprise three housewives, two social workers, two university research staff, one university administrator, one senior community nurse and one retired psychiatrist. All volunteers undergo a selection interview and irrespective of their previous experience participate in the training programme, which is conducted by the Development Officer, helped by members of the Centre Committee and experienced volunteers. The training programme takes place over a ten week period meeting once a week for two and a half to three hours. The following constitute the principal topics: orientation in the aims and objectives of the Centre; familiarisation with its administrative procedures; coping with specific problems; practice in the use of the information bank; theory and practice of basic interviewing and counselling. All volunteers are encouraged to examine their own attitudes and biases towards certain problems and it is understood that if they are unsuitable or find the work uncongenial they will withdraw from the Centre.

Once a counsellor is functioning at the Centre support and supervision is provided at the end of each session. Counsellors use an hour for debriefing each other on the problems they have encountered. These debriefing sessions have the dual benefit of providing support for volunteers while at the same time allowing others to share in considering problems which they themselves may not have confronted in a counselling situation. There is no hierarchy in the volunteer groups; all are considered to be of equal importance and all have a unique contribution to make. Occasional training workshops for volunteers, dealing with specific issues which have arisen in the course of the work, are held at approximately two-monthly intervals.

The Type of Service Offered at the Advice Centre

The Centre has been publicised in a number of different ways: through posters displayed in doctors' waiting rooms, public libraries, community centres, hospitals, supermarkets, the university and colleges etc. In addition, since September 1984 a short advertisement has appeared in the local press. The publicity emphasises the two kinds of service available: an information service and counselling service. It appeals to people with personal, emotional and mental health problems, offering free, confidential help. Additional publicity has been obtained as a result of the Development Officer talking about the Centre to the media, members of the statutory services, voluntary organisations and community clubs and societies, and by 175 visitors coming to see the functioning Centre.

Some clients ask for information or counselling help over the telephone. Those coming into the Centre approach the receptionist with a specific query about a problem or indicate that they need to talk with someone in private. Information is usually provided in the reception area but the receptionists are sensitive to that style of presentation indicative of a need to talk at length about some underlying anxiety. Since there may be times when all counsellors are occupied, a client in acute distress will be supported by the receptionist until a counsellor is available. Although it is not necessary to have an appointment, initial and follow up appointments can be made by telephone or in person in order to be certain of being seen at a particular time or by a particular volunteer. The disadvantage of operating this system is that during some sessions counsellors are overwhelmed with clients, while during other sessions no-one presents at all. Despite this, the notion of easy access to the service is integral to the objectives of the Centre and will be maintained for as long as possible.

What type of service is offered to clients who ask to talk to someone? The 'therapeutic hour' is not rigidly adhered to. In an atmosphere which is designed to convey warmth, genuineness and empathy, the counsellor will take as much time as is necessary first to encourage the client to explain why he* (*the male pronoun is used throughout for grammatical convenience) has come to the Centre. Exploration of the reasons why the client needs someone to talk to, someone to listen to him, is an essential first step in the counselling process. The emphasis is entirely upon the client defining those areas which he is comfortable in presenting to the counsellor and the agenda in the first instance is entirely dictated by the client's needs. The identification of the cause of problems may take more than one session to elicit. The second part of the counselling process involves the counsellor helping the client to outline options for courses of action he may take in order to effect change in his situation or his feelings. The whole aim of all counselling interviews is to *help the clients to help themselves*. The title 'Advice' Centre was inherited from the early planning stage of the Centre and is in many respects a misnomer. Counsellors never advise clients on what to do about their problems.

An integral part of the training, both preliminary and continuous, is to ensure that counsellors are aware of the nature of the relationship which develops between them and their clients. In their reaction to their clients counsellors are expected to be non-judgmental and accepting of the client and his problems; and to suggest referral to another counsellor in the Centre if he is unable to be genuinely empathic or unbiased. For many, the Rogerian notion of unconditional positive regard is an unrealistic aim in counselling; for most people there are certain kinds of behaviour with which they cannot empathise. Counsellors remain sensitive to the undesirability of clients becoming over-dependent. Oldfield summarises succinctly the basic paradox upon which counselling work in this context rests:

> '...that is, that the counsellor offers the client an opportunity for security and detachment, in the full expectation that this experience will lead to increased autonomy' [10].

She quotes Bowlby who stresses:

> 'Self reliance grows from opportunities to rely on others and not be let down; freedom and autonomy are integrally linked with capacities for, and experiences based on, trust and detachment.'

With this emphasis in the work of the Mental Health Advice Centre there is little danger of the client developing feelings of over-dependence upon the counsellor without that person becoming aware of this.

The Centre is not designed to offer long term counselling. When a client has visited on six occasions, the Development Officer and some of the volunteers, including the counsellor involved, review the work that is being carried out in order to ascertain whether or not the Centre is the most appropriate place for that person. If a client clearly requires professional intervention the counsellor will be asked to suggest an appropriate person to whom the client may go for more specialised help.

Confidentiality is a key concept adhered to by all counsellors, whether they are involved in providing information or counselling. This is achieved in a number of different ways. No information about clients is passed on to any other agency, other than at their own request, and where possible in their presence. Counsellors undertake not to discuss their clients or their problems with anyone at all outside the Centre, without the express approval of the client. Discussion of clients' problems among counsellors is confined to the debriefing sessions. Should a counsellor feel that the client would be better helped in some other context he will suggest this as one of the options open to the client; there is no question of counsellors *referring* clients to other agencies.

Only limited records are kept of client contacts with the Centre. For evaluative purposes a Callers Day Book is kept which records all contacts. For clients undergoing counselling, a brief record is kept of the nature of their presenting problem/s, the kind of work undertaken in the counselling interview and what other informal or statutory services they had already contacted in connection with their problem/s. Notes, only identifiable by a code number, are locked and retained within the Centre; access to these is open only to the Development Officer, who is responsible for record keeping, and any counsellors involved in analysing the data for training or evaluative purposes.

There are certain categories of client with whom the Centre does not feel able to work. Those undergoing counselling or psychotherapy with another agency constitute one category (although information will be provided in response to specific enquiries). It was recognised also that it would be impractical to develop expertise in dealing with legal questions or the intricacies of social security. Instead, familiarity with the work of other specialist agencies dealing specifically with such areas enables counsellors to offer information about them and their location to clients. Liaison is a reciprocal process; clients have been sent to the Centre by a range of other voluntary agencies, including the Samaritans and the Citizens' Advice Bureau; a few professionals – general practitioners, psychiatrists and community based social workers have recommended the Centre to some of their patients and clients.

In summary then, the service offered by the Centre is twofold: (a) an information service about other agencies and sources of help and about particular problem areas, with special reference to mental health issues; and (b) a counselling service, either by telephone or individually at the Centre, taking the form of one or several sessions and aimed at helping the client to articulate his areas of concern and to decide for himself, in a supportive, warm atmosphere, what he is going to do to help himself.

The Clients

a) Numbers using the Centre

The number of clients using the Centre and the total number of visits or contacts made by them during the first 18 months of opening is shown in Table 1. The figures in parenthesis give the totals for the first year when the Centre was open for only three sessions each week. Although the actual numbers have

TABLE 1

Number of clients and visits to advice centre

August 1983 – February 1985

(Figures in parentheses refer to August 1983 – August 1984)

	NUMBER OF CLIENTS			NUMBER OF VISITS/CONTACTS		
	Men	Women	Total	Men	Women	Total
Counselling at Centre	105 (38)	214 (75)	319 (113)	242 (94)	289 (123)	531 (217)
Information at Centre	105 (55)	82 (38)	187 (93)	116 (55)	88 (40)	204 (95)
Telephone Counselling	10 (6)	90 (22)	100 (28)	10 (6)	96 (23)	106 (29)
Telephone Information	80 (20)	265 (91)	345 (111)	90 (25)	289 (97)	379 (122)
Total	300 (119)	651 (226)	951 (345)	458 (180)	762 (283)	1220 (463)

risen sharply since the increase in opening hours, the rate of contact per session has remained the same.

More clients used the Centre as an information resource (56 per cent) than availed themselves of counselling (44 per cent) although the proportion of work carried out was 52 per cent counselling, 48 per cent information giving. This apparent discrepancy is accounted for by counselled clients attending more often than those requiring information. Of those engaged in counselling, 63 per cent attended once only; 34 per cent came for between two and five counselling interviews and the remaining 3 per cent received six or more counselling sessions. As counselling invariably takes longer than the mere dispersal of information, it follows that a far greater proportion of *staff time* at the Centre is spent in counselling than information giving. The nature of the counselling, however, is obviously not long term or in-depth for the majority of clients.

Just over twice as many women as men used the Centre. More men than women came into the Centre for information while over three times as many women as men made telephone enquiries. Nine times as many women as men were counselled over the telephone. These sex differences in use of the Centre may, in part, be accounted for by more women being available or having access to a telephone during the hours of opening. Evidence available elsewhere suggests that a higher proportion of women than men experience stress-related symptoms, consult GPs about emotional disorders and are identified by doctors as having conditions that are emotional in origin [16]. The findings therefore may reflect these trends.

b) Occupational Status of Clients who were Counselled

Data on occupational status were obtained from 78 per cent of clients who were counselled. Of these, 48 per cent of the men and 69 per cent of the women were not employed. Ten per cent of the men and 7 per cent of the women were retired, 38 per cent of the men and 20 per cent of the women were registered unemployed while 42 per cent of the women were housewives. These findings may reflect the well-documented prevalence of stress in unemployed people and they may, also, reflect the considerable amount of free time available to people who are not employed.

Of those clients who were employed, equal proportions of men and women (20 per cent) were students. More women, however, were in higher status occupations than the men: 69 per cent of women and 37 per cent of men were in professional, managerial or non-manual jobs: 12 per cent of women and 43 per cent of men were manual workers. It is difficult to account for this discrepancy in occupational status without a more detailed analysis of the inter-relationships between gender, age, marital status and type of presentational problem, which is beyond the scope of this paper.

c) Other help sought

A preliminary analysis of other help previously sought with the problems presented at the Centre was confined to examining contact with general practitioners, social workers and the psychiatric services. Two-fifths of all counselled clients had consulted their general practitioners; social workers had been approached by 13 per cent and one-fifth of the clients had been in contact with the psychiatric services. These findings suggest that the help provided by these statutory services for these clients was felt by them to be either inadequate or inappropriate.

Although the Centre was established primarily for clients who had never received psychiatric treatment, one-third of all counselled clients had at some stage in their lives been in contact with the psychiatric services. This proportion is the same as that reported by the Isis Centre [10] and suggests that the Crown Street Centre has a role to play in rehabilitation as well as prevention.

d) Kinds of Problems Presented

A preliminary analysis of the problems presented by a small sample of the counselled clients (one in five of the men and one in ten of the women) has been completed. On average each client presented three problems during counselling. When these were categorised into main problems and subsidiary or emergent problems, it was found that of the main problems 82 per cent were emotional and 18 per cent practical, while of the subsidiary problems 63 per cent were emotional and 37 per cent practical. Overall, there were no sex differences.

A closer examination of these problems shows that those presented by the highest proportion of men (56 per cent) are equally anxiety and/or depression, and an alcohol related problem, followed by other psychological symptoms (50 per cent) with marital problems presented by 44 per cent. The most common problem presented by women was marital (61 per cent), followed by anxiety and/or depression (56 per cent) and equally 44 per cent reported housing, financial problems and loneliness.

A further analysis of all counselled clients shows that 4 per cent of men and 13 per cent of women presented with problems related to their being 'carers' of dependent relatives. Of these, 40 per cent of the male's dependents and 57 per cent of the female's dependents had been in contact with the psychiatric services. Although the total numbers are small, there is clearly a role for counselling services to support carers of the mentally ill, as proposed by SSHD [12]. These very crude, preliminary findings suggest that there *is* an unmet need in this community for help with emotional problems.

THE FUTURE DEVELOPMENT OF THE CENTRE

The work of the Centre may develop in a number of different ways. The information and counselling service could be expanded, in response to perceived need, which may include opening during the weekend or for further evening sessions. The Centre is actively considering 'outeach'. When the present trainee counsellors have completed their initial orientation there will be sufficient trained staff to consider placing some volunteers in settings other than the centrally situated Advice Centre. For example, 'clinics' could be held in local community centres, providing a similar service to that offered in the Advice Centre on perhaps a weekly basis. Volunteers would be supported by staff at the Centre and would have access to the resources of information and personal support and supervision available at Crown Street.

Members of the public would thereby be given an opportunity to seek help with their emotional problems on a local basis. There are certain people, of course, who will continue to prefer the anonymity of a central service.

The Centre is already being used as a pre-training experiential resource for some students about to embark upon the University Diploma Course in Social Work. Pre-students are encouraged to spend time working in both the Day Centre and the Advice Centre in order to gain experience that may not be readily available elsewhere. This use of the Centre could be expanded so that ultimately it would provide a source of placement for social work students, community psychiatric nurses in training and possibly also other professional groups.

Most of the work carried out in the Centre at present is individual and there is considerable scope for development of group work; already one volunteer whose particular skills and experience lie in the use of relaxation techniques is holding a weekly relaxation class for appropriate clients presenting to the Day Centre and Advice Centre. In this way the Centre is able to provide time and space for volunteers with particular interests so long as these are consistent with the aims and objectives of the Association. It is hoped that eventually drama therapy, music therapy and some form of art therapy may also be possible.

Following the three year initial experiment period, and subject to successfully obtaining funding from statutory services thereafter, the Centre could provide a resource to which professional workers are seconded on a part time basis in order to exercise their own particular discipline in a community context. The Isis Centre, since its inception in 1970, has been staffed by professional psychiatrists, psychologists, social workers, nurses and clergy, who spend part of one day each week working at the Centre. The Isis Centre also uses volunteers to a limited extent [10]. It would not be impossible for attached professional workers to work alongside the volunteers at the Advice Centre. Plans are already under way to expand the existing part time Day Centre so that it is open for eight sessions during the week and one session during the weekend.

At the time of writing, the Centre has funds to support itself for the final year of the experimental period. Despite the fact that 'voluntary organisations have a central role to play in the organisation and provision of community care', they 'in this as in every other field, labour under financial difficulties', in particular 'by the short term nature of most of their statutory funding' [17]. The Association is pursuing actively the acquisition of further funding from a variety of sources, and plans for the development of the Centre are proceeding in the hope that some support will be obtained. The case should be strengthened by the evaluation presently being carried out.

The Centre as a co-ordinated unit is providing both a preventive and rehabilitative mental health service in this community. The Advice Centre, in providing an information and counselling service, is responding to the needs of those who have and have not received psychiatric care, and whose emotional distress is not being alleviated elsewhere. Simultaneously, the Day Centre is providing rehabilitative day care and social support for former psychiatric patients. As such the Crown Street Centre is attempting to meet some of the needs identified by SHHD in Mental Health in Focus [17]. Or, as an Advice Centre client, now attending the Day Centre, put it succinctly: 'If there'd been a place like this years ago, I'd never have got into this state. But now I'm here, you're helping me to help myself get back on my feet again' [18].

References

1. Goldberg, D. & Huxley, P. *Mental Illness in the Community: the Pathway to Psychiatric Care.* Tavistock, London, 1980.

2. Brown, G.W. & Harris, T. *Social Origins of Depression: A Study of Psychiatric Disorder in Women.* Tavistock, London, 1978.

3. Robinson, D. & Henry, S. *Self-Help and Health*. Martin Robertson, London, 1977.

4. Buchan, I.C. & Richardson, I.M. *Time Study of Consultations: in General Practice*. Scottish Health Service Studies No.27, Scottish Home & Health Department, Edinburgh, 1973.

5. Butler, R. *How Many Patients?* Occasional Paper on Social Administration, No.64, Bedford Square Press, London, 1980.

6. Williams, P., Murray, J. & Clare, A.W. 'A Longitudinal Study of Psychotropic Drug Prescription' *Psychological Medicine*. 12, 1982, 201-6.

7. Coleman, V. *Life Without Tranquilisers*. Piatkus Ltd, London, 1985.

8. Furlong, R.C.S., Brough, D.I. & Watson, J.P. 'Lewisham Mental Health Advice Centre: A New Development in Community Care' *Community Development Journal*. 18, 3, 1983, 224-30.

9. Hargreaves, R. 'Brindle House – A Community Mental Health Service in Practice'. In Reed, J. & Loms, G. *Psychiatric Services in the Community*. Croom Helm, London, 1984, 171-7.

10. Oldfield, S. *The Counselling Relationship*. Routledge & Kegan Paul, London, 1983.

11. Lazare, A., Eisenthal, S. & Wasserman, L. 'The Customer Approach to Patienthood: Attending to Patient Requests in a Walk-in Clinic' *Activities of General Psychiatry*. 32, 1975, 553-8.

12. Mental Health in Focus, SHHD, Edinburgh, 1985.

13. Truax, C.B. & Mitchell, K.M. 'Research on Certain Therapist Interpersonal Skills in Relation to Process and Outcome'. In Bergin, A.E. & Garfield, S.L. *Handbook of Psycho-therapy and Behaviour Change*. Wiley, New York, 1971.

14. Aberdeen and North East Association for Mental Health, Annual Report, 1984.

15. Meichenbaum, D. & Jaremko, M.E. (Eds.) *Stress Reduction and Prevention*. Plenum Press, New York & London, 1983.

16. Horowitz, A. 'The Pathways into Psychiatric Treatment: Some Differences Between Men and Women' *J. Health & Soc. Beh*. 18, 1977, 169-178.

17. Short Report. Second Report from the Social Services Committee: Community Care Vol.1, HMSO, London, 985.

18. Case material.

Politics and Psychiatry: The Case of Italy

S.P.W. Brown

INTRODUCTION

It is generally acknowledged that something momentous has happened to the mental health services in Italy. A system of institutional care has been turned into (or is being turned into) an effective community care system. Behind these changes is a distinctive meeting of politics and psychiatry. Indeed, *Psichiatrica Democratica*, the name of the group of radical mental health workers influential in promoting the abrupt change in policy in 1978, is synonymous with the kind of community psychiatric care now being offered.

Political psychiatry in Italy has not only the meaning that psychiatrists, social workers, nurses and volunteers are involved in (left) political activity. It has the connotation, as well, that a form of psychiatry is practised which has its origins in socialist/marxist views of power and social relations as well as (or even in the place of) psychiatric categories of diagnosis and therapy. It is clearly beyond the scope of this paper to trace either the straightforwardly political impact of psichiatrica democratica on the policy process or the connections between political theory and the critique of orthodox psychiatry advanced by them. Instead, I have a more modest aim. I wish to review the Italian experience as a critical case to be set beside some current concerns about the development of community psychiatric care in Britain.

The two caveats must be entered immediately. In the first place, the intention is not to celebrate the Italian reforms in a reprise of the heady talk (but not much action) of the anti-psychiatric kind most pronounced in the 1960s and 1970s. Reception of the Italian reforms has been mixed and, since the evidence about their effects is very patchy, rather cautious conclusions about the benefits of political psychiatry must be drawn. Secondly, and relatedly, the argument is not that straightforward lessons about policy change or radical mental health care can be drawn from Italy, as if what happened there might be grafted into the British scene. Experiments do not travel well in that sense; the differences between socio-political structures, cultures and, importantly in this case, professional cultures are too great. The question which the paper addresses is rather this: what issues about the policies and politics of community mental health care does the Italian experience open up? Whether or not the reforms in Italy are successful, the issues remain and they are ones which need to be placed on the agenda in Britain.

These issues are organised around two different views of recent social welfare policies. The first is concerned with the denial of care in the community: the view that community care is a rhetoric which masks the dumping (or leaving) of people in need in hostile neighbourhoods. This is the most familiar talking point in the community care debate. But a second view points critically at the received wisdom about preventing dumping. The issues raised here have to do with the increasing levels of regulation and supervision which result from the activities of welfare agencies. Community care, here, is regarded as an extension of control and discipline. Let us see how the Italian experience addresses these issues.

THE ITALIAN MENTAL HEALTH ACT

In 1978 legislation was passed in Italy with the remarkably radical purpose of replacing hospital psychiatric care with a community based service. Its main provisions were these:

(1) No new psychiatric patients were to be admitted to state mental hospitals and, after 1 January 1981, no patients could be re-admitted;

(2) Construction of new psychiatric hospitals or wards was prohibited;

(3) Hospital psychiatric wards of no more than 15 beds per health catchment area (the *unita saniteria locale*) were permitted; they were to be linked to 'alternative structures' in the community, principally 'psycho-social centres'; (USLs contain between 100,000 to 120,000 people);

(4) While compulsory admissions were, in certain circumstances, permitted, they were subject to judicial review and the decision open to appeal.

Since its enactment, Reform Law No 180 has been incorporated in a general health measure, Law 833.

Reform Law 180 represents an achievement in getting mental health issues on the political agenda. Tactically, it arose from a threat by the relatively small Radical Party (supported by about 5 per cent of the electorate) to call a referendum on existing mental health laws in the 1978 general election. The political significance of such a move was that the governing Christian Democrat and Communist coalition parties had been recently surprised by a referendum liberalising divorce laws. A 'successful' referendum on the mental health issue would have rendered invalid existing legislation and, importantly, the funding arrangements of the psychiatric service. As Jones and Poletti [1] describe it, the threat of a referendum had the effect of rushing new legislation through the Italian Parliament in the seemingly record time of 23 days. Mosher [2] indicates that Franco Basaglia (whose work and writing, as we shall see, were a crucial influence on the reform movement) was closely involved in drafting the act.

However, the reforms were not really an affair of a political shotgun at the heads of the major parties. There was broad political support for liberalising the mental health system. In particular, a 'stormy courtship' between Psichiatrica Democratica and the Communist Party had resulted in the Party adopting mental health reform on its political platform [2]. Indeed, the reforms cannot be understood without reference to the convergence between psychiatry and politics in Italy over the two decades leading up to the legislation itself.

The politicisation of psychiatry in Italy has been described elsewhere [3] [4] [5]. The accounts suggest an increasingly critical view of institutional treatment of all kinds and, in parallel, the view that psychiatric problems and therapeutic relationships (between doctors or nurses and patients) were inexorably tied up with political relations of power. Basaglia wrote of an early effort to change institutional psychiatry:

> 'Basic to the psychiatrist's traditional role, and obscured by the aura of scientific objectivity, was the task of isolating and containing social problems and conflicts.....Thus, the attack on (the institutional) system was not just a theoretical critique, but a political intervention − a fact amply brought home by the obstructions and aggravations experienced from the powers that be.'

Basaglia's work (here the experimental Gorizia project) is taken by Crepet and De Plato [4] as being a first stage in the process leading to the reforms. At

Gorizia, Basaglia took over a psychiatric hospital of some 800 beds in 1961. The changes which he inaugurated resembled in many respects the therapeutic community style of treatment. Indeed, Basaglia had worked with Maxwell Jones, possibly the best known exponent of the therapeutic community approach [7]. However, Basaglia and the workers around him regarded the therapeutic community as an attempt 'to make the asylum work better' − not so at Gorizia, where the purpose was 'to lay the groundwork for its total destruction' [6]. By 1968, the patient population at Gorizia had dropped to about 350, during a period when there was no marked reduction in the overall numbers of patients in hospital psychiatric care [2].

Crepet and De Plato's marking of the end of this demonstration period of alternatives to the existing system of Italian psychiatry (and including not only Basaglia's work, but the attempted adoption of French 'secteurisation' − or neighbourhood psychiatry − and of the American community mental health centres [8]) in 1968 is, of course, a reflection of the political and cultural upheavals at the end of the 1960s:

> '...in 1968, not only were factories and universities occupied but also mental hospitals. In the people's consciousness, the inmates of psychiatric hospitals were viewed as the most unprotected element of the subordinate classes and it was considered that they should be offered solidarity and attention' [4].

In terms of the spread of political psychiatry in Italy, the few years after 1968 saw Basaglia-type reforms in a number of psychiatric hospitals. Basaglia himself moved to Trieste hospital in 1971 and similar projects were mounted in Perugia, Arrezzo, Regio Emilia and Naples. The relatively informal network of psychiatrists and mental health workers involved in the reform of institutional regimes was consolidated in 1974 by the formation of the Society for Democratic Psychiatry (Psichiatrica Democratica). Between 1976 (the first national convention of Psichiatrica Democratica) and 1978 considerable political activity took place, both locally with the administrations of local government in the areas where institutions were being reformed, and nationally − notably, the 'stormy courtship' of the Communist Party mentioned above. However, while the ideas and work of the reform movement were undoubtedly given sympathetic attention in political circles, it took the straightforward adoption of democratic psychiatric principles by the Radical Party to prompt the national legislation.

This potted version of policy change is, for obvious reasons, inadequate. It is intended to do no more than to point to the linking of a theoretical and practical critique of institutional psychiatry with left political activity in the period leading to the reforms. The linkage is clear in the manifesto statement of Psichiatrica Democratica. It is a programmatic statement, talking of segregation and institutional repression, 'the corporative, speculative and bureaucratic logic of the current health system', and the need to co-operate with worker organisations [9]. The political alignment is fairly straightforward: to belong to Psichiatrica Democratica (or to be associated with it) is to espouse leftist politics. Psychiatry and politics are openly intertwined in Italy.

POLITICS AND PSYCHIATRY: AN ASIDE

A slight detour is appropriate here to establish a theme to be developed later in the paper. It has to do with this explicit convergence of politics and psychiatry in Italy. In some respects this seems to be like the swingeing attacks on orthodox psychiatry by the anti-psychiatry movement in Britain, France and the United States during the 1960s and early 1970s. There, too, the critique of the institution and of professional mystification was associated with various kinds of libertarianism – of the right in the case of Thomas Szasz [10] or of the left in the case of Foucault [11]. Indeed, Jones and Poletti mention that Basaglia attempted to convene an international forum consisting of the anti-psychiatry *célèbres* – Goffman, Foucault, Szasz and Laing. They remark, drily, that the group never met [12]. Now, it is nicely ironic that these figures are precisely the object of Sedgewick's impressive and highly critical book about politics and psychiatry [13]. He makes the point that the politics of the anti-psychiatry movement were never coherent and often (say, with Laing) highly ambiguous. His biting argument is that the attack on institutional and largely state-provided psychiatry gives a justification for 'the advancing counter-revolution of welfare cutbacks and other dilapidations decreed by rightward-moving governments in the present period of recession and militarisation' (p.245).

Sedgewick's attack on the politics of anti-psychiatry is that the intellectual critique never develops into a set of concrete demands for an alternative strategy. It is a similar point to that made by Turkle [14] that, in France, much anti-psychiatry is really intellectual and social play, 'actings-out of nostalgia for the (1968) May days (which) may be keeping the French anti-psychiatric movement lively, but may also be undercutting its productivity as a meaningful political struggle' (p.177). By contrast, of course, in Italy the critical ideas (and psychiatric practice) of Psichiatrica Democratica did develop as a political practice.

The significance of the point is that the way the Italian reforms are viewed (especially, as we shall see below, since their empirical documentation is thus far rather limited) is influenced by the way one sees the meshing of politics and psychiatry there. Thus, Sedgewick, generally intolerant of the 'romantic irredentism' of anti-psychiatry, does regard Psichiatrica Democratica as producing a sensible and practical alternative to institutional and professionally-dominated psychiatry. Other commentators see the movement as the unwarranted interference of the social administration of mental health care by socialist or marxist tendencies.

WHAT HAS HAPPENED IN CONSEQUENCE?

Two very different versions of the consequences of the 1978 legislation have been reported. In one, the closure of hospitals and the opening of psycho-social centres are seen as a major achievement in mental health care. Certainly, the process of deinstitutionalising psychiatric services is not yet complete. Of the 55,000 state hospital psychiatric patients in 1978, it is frequently asserted that about 35,000 still remain in hospital. Nevertheless, some commentators regard the development of services in the community as ably coping with the effects of deinstitutionalisation policies.

Mosher [2] is of the opinion that the Italian legislation is 'the most comprehensive community-oriented mental health act in the Western industrialised world' (p.199). She reports that there has been no evidence of 'dumping' and no increase in suicide or violent crime by former patients. She declares that an 18 per cent decrease in the number of state hospital inpatients and a 60 per cent reduction in compulsory admissions has not been accompanied by an increased rate of admissions to private hospitals. She does not say how the statistics on which her conclusions are based were gathered. As we shall see, there is a major problem here.

Ramon [5] studied the workings of one mental health service in an Italian town of about 50,000 inhabitants. As a background to her intensive study to the service, she reports that there were no hospital admissions from the town between 1978 and 1981 and only eight re-admissions during 1981; and these into the wards of the small general hospital which serves the town. However, the value of her study is the description of the working methods of the inter-disciplinary community psychiatric team. She gives a picture of a rather relaxed and domiciliary-type service in which considerable attempts are made to be informal, both with respect to the dealings of team members with clients and among the team itself. Other accounts within this generally favourable mould speak of the buoyant mood in the psycho-social centres where clients come for company, a meal and group discussion about mutual problems [15,16]. There is an emphasis, here, on the lack of formal psychiatric classification of patients or formal treatment programmes. Both these aspects are, of course, implications of the critique of orthodox psychiatric practice by Psichiatrica Democratica.

The picture of the Italian reforms offered here has been reproduced in a number of recent articles in the nursing and social work press. Thus, the deputy director of MIND wrote of an exhibition organised by the Psichiatrica Democratica group that it showed how 'Italy has managed to make care in the community a living reality' [17]. The community service teams have been praised as being 'collectivist (and) non-hierarchical (which) seem to have abandoned traditional roles' [18]. And a recent television programme offered a similarly favourable picture of the policy [19]. The Italian experience, then, is presented by some as a strategy for achieving non-institutional psychiatric care quite alternative to the faltering and uncertain attempts in Britain. As one of the academic advocates of Italian democratic psychiatry argues, in Britain the commitment to community mental health care is superficial both in political and professional circles; by contrast, the reforms in Italy had broad political support orchestrated to a large extent by the Psichiatrica Democratica movement [5].

In contrast to these (albeit limited) reports of Italian community services, Jones and Poletti have recently mounted a critical attack [1]. Their version of what has happened since 1978 raises important questions about the documentation (or lack of it) of the consequences of the reforms. They question, for example, the definitional adequacy, as well as the analysis of the statistics which show the one-third drop in hospital patients since the legislation. Some patients remaining in hospital are designated as 'guests' and are not officially counted; psychogeriatric patients are not included in the psychiatric registers, but on geriatric registers; patients in private hospitals are not counted on a national level, thus casting some doubt on Mosher's conclusion that private hosital admissions have not increased since the 1978 legislation [1]. They cite the beginning work of Torre and Marinoni in setting up small area case-registers indicating psychiatric need [20] [21], although, as they say, hard data which possess some explanatory power are hard to come by.

The reports of their own study tour of the community service system is particularly critical. Only one psycho-social centre, for example, approximated to the descriptions of Ramon and others. 'Elsewhere, the CPS was basically a formal outpatient clinic. Here patients came by appointment, saw their psychiatrist, received their prescription and left' [22]. Psycho-social centres are none the worse for being like British outpatient clinics; the point is that Jones and Poletti are doubtful about their being the egalitarian milieux celebrated elsewhere. They conclude:

> '... the law (has) operated very patchily, and while some of the staff we met in areas with Communist administrations were enthusiastic about its possibilities, the overwhelming consensus was that the law would have to be changed because it was unworkable' [22].

For these commentators, the real lessons of the Italian experience are that large scale mental hospital closure plans do not work.

In view of the paucity of the published evidence (precisely the point that Jones and Poletti make) it seems rather extravagant for either side to draw the conclusions they do. On empirical grounds the issues are still open. Quite clearly, we do not know the rate at which hospital patients are being discharged, where they are going to, what their lives are like wherever they are going to and (as is increasingly an issue in the feminist-inspired critique of British community care policies) what the lives of their families or relatives (for which, read women [23]) are like if they go there. Nor do we know what the lives of the 35,000 (and maybe inaccurately counted) patients remaining in hospital are like; Jones and Poletti give a grim, but necessarily impressionistic picture. Nor is the extent of need in the community (whether that of discharged patients or of people never in the institutional system) known. Nor, finally, do we know to what extent the critique of psychiatric hospitals and institutionalisation developed by Psichiatrica Democratica has actually been translated into different kinds of social relations or helping strategies in the developing community service sector.

While the answers to these kinds of questions are, ultimately, the tests of the success of the Italian reforms, this should not prevent a different sort of appraisal being made in the meantime. And it is this which returns us to the points made above about the meeting between politics and psychiatry. For, whatever the eventual merits or limitations of the efforts to close Italian psychiatric hospitals, it is clear that the debate there is conducted in very different terms from the one in Britain. In Italy, the politicisation of psychiatry opened it up to views about the relationships between the patient, the doctor and the state quite outside the bounds of traditional psychiatric discourse.

POLITICAL PSYCHIATRY AND THE COMMUNITY CARE DEBATE

As we have seen, Basaglia's view of psychiatry is that it maintains public order ('by isolating and containing social problems and conflicts') behind the mask of scientific objectivity [6]. One practical implication of this was the linking of the progressive grouping of mental health workers (organised around the Psichiatrica Democratica movement) with other more straightforwardly (progressive) political interests – political parties, trades unions and local (communist) administrations. That these links were necessary and effective in changing the system and practice of psychiatry in Italy can be seen in the success of the reform movement in putting mental health on the political agenda. It can also be seen in the *form* of the community mental health service which is developing, and this notwithstanding Jones and Poletti's reservations. For there seems to be a confusion in their reports about whether collectivist, non-hierarchical community services are desirable *per se* or whether it is a question of the limited extent of such forms. If the latter, then clearly there is no disagreement between them and the advocates of the Italian experience – although, of course, there is still the critical question of whether such forms can be made more widespread. Crepet and De Plato [4], as well as Jones and Poletti, both point to the countervailing tendencies among traditionally oriented psychiatrists and health administrators, and to the familiar issue of financing community care development. Completing the process of reform will no doubt be arduous. But, if the disagreement is about the kind of democratic psychiatry being practised then there is less chance of a reconciliation. Let me unpack this issue by considering what deserves to be called the 'great debate' about decarceration.

The terms of the academic discussion about the closure of institutions (prisons and reformatories, as well as hospitals) are, of course, set by Scull's provocative book *Decarceration* [24]. He uses the term as a shorthand for 'the state-sponsored policy for closing down asylums, prisons and reformatories'(p.1). Part of his argument is the now widely known political economic critique of why this happened. That is, in the place of explanations which concentate on liberalising institutional and segregative treatment, he offers the fiscal crisis of the state. Without unduly caricaturing his argument, it is a case of institutions being the victim of the rising rate of state expenditure and the desire to curb it.

Scull's argument has been extensively criticised [25,26,27]. Busfield, in particular, points to the implausibility of an account which relies so heavily on the economic problems of the State at a time when there has been a marked increase in welfare activity. Against Scull, she shows that growth has occurred in the provision of day hospitals, outpatient clinics and psychiatric units in general hospitals:

> 'These changes are part of what has been called the growth of the therapeutic state and represents both an enormous expansion of psychiatric activity, most of which in this country is provided by the State and an important change in the character of the services provided and the patients dealt with. In the face of this expansion an explanation that concentrates on the *reduced* costs of deinstitutionalisation has little *prima facie* validity' [25, p.6].

A similar criticism is offered in the case of penal strategies, another instance of the supposed decarcerative thrust [28] [29].

Notwithstanding the objections to the historical accuracy (and to the theoretical limitations) of his argument, Scull's views about the results of decarcerative policies connect with a widespread concern about the fate of patients in the community. He has a bleak view of community care – or, rather, the denial of care in the community. Some of the decanted patients may:

> '...blend unobtrusively back into the communities from whence they came.....but for many other ex-inmates and potential inmates, the alternative to the institution has been to be herded into newly emerging 'deviant ghettoes', sewers of human misery and what is conventionally defined as social pathology within which (largely hidden from outside inspection or even notice) society's refuse may be repressively tolerated' [24, p.1-2].

It is precisely this vision of miserable, exploited and marginalised people not being cared for at all in the community which lies behind the anxiety about rapid hospital closures. But, and it is an important but, the debate about how to prevent such dumping, whether carried on in political or professional circles, has concentrated almost exclusively on finding ways of surrounding people in need with new kinds of professional or administrative control. Thus, one upshot of all the talk of helping mentally disordered people to lead independent and socially integrated lives in the community is the network of day centres and hostels, staffed by local authority workers who are encouraged to think of themselves (largely unrealistically) as professional workers.

Let me draw a distinction here between institutionalisation and institutionism. It may clarify the limitations of the debate about community care to which I am pointing. Institutionalisation is, of course, the familiar target of dissatisfaction with mental hospitals. It refers, essentially, to the characteristics of particularly stilted and oppressive forms of social relationships and to their consequences on people's sense of themselves and their actions. The classic account is Goffman's *Asylums* [30]. Institutionism is the belief that the damage which is done by such stilted and oppressive social relationships is restricted to those places we commonly call institutions – notably, hospitals, prisons and the like. The belief has a point to it. It is in places like hospitals that social relations are conducted in terms of 'block' treatment and large social distances between staff and inmates. But that does not happen only in such places, and to confuse institutionalisation with institutionism is to confuse a form (or a 'modality', to use Cohen's term [28]) of controlled social relationships with a site of social control. Sedgewick, in this context, observes that:

> 'the politicisation of psychiatry has been unique in the degree of attention that it has afforded to the character of the hospital itself as an agency for worsening pathology, for manufacturing it where it does not exist or for operating it as an extra-judiciary means of incarceration against those who have scorned official mores' [13, p.197].

That is to say, in the context of this argument, the debate is levelled at places where patients are oppressed. But it is to miss the point (the point of my distinction) that it is not places but forms of social relationships which are oppressive. Of course, within hospitals (and prisons and public schools, to include other examples of the total institution) such relationships flourish and have their historical origin. But the new concern is that they are extending from those sites in the guise of professional and administrative care. It is the point that Busfield [25] referred to by mentioning the 'therapeutic state'.

The argument which develops from this point is most tellingly put by Foucault [31]. It is organised around his notion of 'the carceral', that is to say, the principles and practices which contribute to social discipline. They include detailed classifications of people, minutely analysed programmes of training and extensive supervision or surveillance. His argument is this: these forms of discipline originated in prisons, military barracks, schools and hospitals during the late 18th and early 19th centuries. But (and much more recently) these forms of discipline have spread outwards from the institutions themselves to regulate a wide range of social activity. Foucault's argument centres on the prison. But the theme is taken up in the context of mental health by Castel et al [8]. They suggest that the development of community mental health care policies may be seen as a changing strategy of psychiatry, such that it takes on responsibility not only for the treatment of florid abnormality within mental hospitals, but less obvious (and more morally than pathologically judged) kinds in society at large.

In a review article of Castel's argument, Miller suggests that psychiatry is in the process of 'renegotiating a social territory'. That is, psychiatric thinking and practice

'...are able to operate through a variety of sites which include the school, the family, social work, doctors and psychiatrists' [32, p.98].

The point of this excursion is that the debate about community care is not only addressed to the problem of preventing people from being dumped into the community or wandering Scull's deviant ghettoes. It is also about counteracting the spread of the 'disseminated forms of the carceral network' [31]. And it is this concern (although not in the same language) which prompted the development of political psychiatry in Italy with its principles of collectivist, non-hierarchical organisation.

SO WHAT?

What then, is to be made of the Italian experience, as incomplete as it is and as inadequately evaluated as it is? Let me return to Sedgewick's comments about politics and psychiatry. His concerns, it will be remembered, were that the spate of anti-psychiatry writing in the 1960s and early 1970s never developed into a systematic alternative strategy to state-provided, professionally dominated and largely hospital-located psychiatry. In one respect, his critique is too harsh for his concluding positive proposals about a more practical political psychiatry to bear. Burton (1983) comments, exactly along the lines that Sedgewick argues, that 'it is worth stressing the importance of a clear programme, or of an image of a possible way of providing services', but then charges Sedgewick with naivety:

'Sedgewick naively seizes on an amalgam of the Mental After Care Association, Kropotkin's anarchist critique of the State and the Belgian village of Geel where 5.8 per cent of Belgium's mentally ill people board with families, accounting for 5 per cent of Geel's population and suffer some exploitation and widespread discrimination' [33, p.71].

He cites an article by Shearer [34] on this last point.

This is to do something of a disservice to Sedgewick, because he does rather more than this. What he argues for is a broad alliance of mental health workers (both in the hospital and social services sector), patients' organisations (of which the Mental Patients Union is an example) and relatives and friends of mentally disordered people. The only problem, as he admits, is that there ae very few signs that such a broad alliance is on the cards in Britain.

The position appears to be very similar across a whole range of welfare issues, for which there is widespread dissatisfaction with the level or kinds of services provided, some incisive writing about the reasons for the political and professional neglect, but little by way of practical radical alternatives. Phillipson [35], for example, discusses the creation of dependency in old age under capitalism. But he observes the lack of a radical socialist policy on such kinds of dependency. In much the same terms, Oliver is somewhat pessimistic about the prospect of physical disability acquiring a positive political significance:

> '...(due to) the lack of (a) coherent political force to articulate the demands of disabled people, any gains are likely to be small-scale and piecemeal. In fact, the real problem in the short term may well be to defend what has already been gained rather than attempt to achieve any real or significant improvements. Those working within the politics of disability will already know that, in fact, this has been the major preoccupation in recent years' [36, p.31].

In the light of such observations about the general prospects of major reform within the welfare system, and, more importantly, in the light of the present political and economic tendencies, which appear to be more concerned with passing the responsibility for care on to families and the private or voluntary sector, than with reforming state-provided care, the Italian experience would seem to have little to offer the British context. But this is to miss the significance of democratic psychiatry in Italy as a demonstration of what can be achieved as an alternative form of mental health care – patchy perhaps, limited and containing unresolved tensions, but nevertheless existent. One strategic significance of the Italian experience is the way in which a set of issues about community care, largely neglected in the current debate, is addressed. That is, how may the mentally disordered be helped without perpetuating the oppressive relationships of the asylum? This is precisely the point of the brand of political psychiatry developed in Italy. As we have seen, the relationship between politics and psychiatry has been not only a case of mental health workers acquiring some political muscle. It has also been a case of mental health practice being permeated with principles of equality and collective action which derive from a socialist political viewpoint.

But the reforms have a second and tactical significance. They stand in the development of community psychiatric care in much the same relation as the ENCOR project stands to the development of services for mentally handicapped people [37] [38]. There, an extant model of an integrated community service for mentally handicapped people fleshed out the arguments of, among others, the Campaign for Mentally Handicapped People in Britain and made them more plausible. This is not, of course, to ignore the need for a critical and systematic evaluation of the consequences of such programmes; nor to be innocently enthusiastic about their own compromises or contradictions. Dalley [39], for example, has commented on the 'famialism' which tends to preoccupy some advocates of ENCOR's pattern of services – a utopian view of family-like relationships between carer and cared for. Similarly, Heginbotham points to the individualistic and unproblematical notion of 'normality' which lies behind the normalisation principle [40]. Nevertheless, with caution and critical examination, the Italian reforms may be seen as a practical alternative to what Jones and Poletti rightly call the impasse in the development of community care in Britain [22].

But the issue is not, as they see it, that the lesson of the Italian reforms is that mental hospitals cannot be abolished and that patients cannot be re-absorbed into the community without pain or effort. It is rather that the development of alternative forms of psychiatric care requires political muscle as well as incisive ideas. Psichiatrica Democratica is a useful example.

References

1. Jones, K. & Poletti, A. 'Transformation of the Asylum: the Italian experience' International Journal of Mental Health. 1985, forthcoming.

2. Mosher, L. 'Italy's Revolutionary Mental Health Law: an assessment' American Journal of Psychiatry. 139(2), 1982, 199-203.

3. Basaglia, F. et al L'Instituzione Negata. Milan, Einandi, 1968. To be republished as The Negative Institution. Routledge & Kegan Paul, London, forthcoming.

4. Crepet, P. & De Plato, G. Psychiatry Without Asylums: origins and prospects in Italy' International Journal of Health Services. 13, 1, 1983, 119-129.

5. Ramon, S. 'Psichiatrica Democratica: a case study of an Italian community mental health service' International Journal of Health Services. 2, 1983, 307-324.

6. Basaglia, F. 'Breaking the Circuit of Control'. In Ingleby, D. (Ed.) Critical Psychiatry. Penguin, Harmondsworth, 1981.

7. Jones, M. Social Psychiatry. London, Tavistock, 1952.

8. Castel, R. et al The Psychiatric Society. Columbia University Press, 1982.

9. Minguzzi, G.F. *Practice of Madness* (preface). Minutes of the First Meeting of Democratic Psychiatry. Gorizia, Italy, 1974.

10. Szasz, T. *The Myth of Mental Illness*. New York, 1961.

11. Foucault, M. *Madness and Civilisation*. Tavistock, London, 1967.

12. *New Society*. 4th October 1984.

13. Sedgewick, P. *Psycho Politics*. Pluto Press, London, 1982.

14. Turkle, S. 'French Anti-psychiatry'. In Ingleby, D. (Ed.) *Critical Psychiatry*. Penguin, Harmondsworth, 1981.

15. Daniels, G. 'One Nurse's Week' *Nursing Mirror*. 11, May 1983, 40.

16. Hanvey, C. 'Italy and the Rise of Democratic Psychiatry' *Community Care*. 25th October 1978, 22-24.

17. Heptinstall, D. 'Psichiatrica Democratica: Italy's revolution in caring for the mentally ill' *Community Care*. 1st March 1984, 17-19.

18. Hicks, C. 'The Italian Experience' *Nursing Times*. 21st March 1984.

19. Italy's Mad Law? Channel 4, 15th March, 1985.

20. Torre, E., Marioni, A. & Allegro, G. 'Loest Psychiatric Case Registers: old and new long stay patients' *Social Psychiatry*. 17, 125.

21. Torre, E., Marioni, A. & associates 'Trends in Admissions before and after the Act Abolishing Mental Hospitals: a survey in three areas of Northern Italy' *Comprehensive Psychiatry*. 23, 3, 1982b, 227.

22. Jones, K. & Poletti, A. 'Understanding the Italian Experience' *British Journal of Psychiatry* (forthcoming).

23. Wilson, E. 'Women, the "Community" and the "Family". In Walker, A. (Ed.) *Community Care*. Blackwell & Robertson, Oxford, 1982.

24. Scull, A. *Decarceration*. Prentice-Hall, Englewood Cliffs, N.J., 1977.

25. Busfield, J. *The Historical Antecedents of Decarceration: the mentally ill*. University of Essex, 1980.

26. Figlio, K. & Jordanova, L. 'Review of Scull, A. Decarceration' *Radical Science Journal*. 8, 1979, 99-104.

27. Matthews, R. '"Decarceration" and the Fiscal Crisis'. In Fine, R. et al (Eds.) *Capitalism and the Rule of Law*. Hutchinson, London, 1979.

28. Cohen, S. 'The Punitive City: notes on the dispersal of social control' *Contemporary Crises*. 3, 1979, 339-363.

29. Hudson, B. 'The Rising Use of Imprisonment: the impact of "decarceration" policies' *Critical Social Policy*. 11, 1984, 46 - 59.

30. Goffman, E. *Asylums*. Penguin, Harmondsworth, 1968.

31. Foucault, M. *Discipline and Punish: Birth of the Prison*. Allen Lane, London, 1977.

32. Miller, P. 'Psychiatry – the Renegotiation of a Territory' *Ideology and Consciousness*. 8, 1981, 97-121.

33. Burton, M. 'Understanding Mental Health Services: Theory and Practice' *Critical Social Policy*. 3, 1983, 54-74.

34. Shearer, A. 'Caring for the Mentally Ill' *New Statesman*. 103, 12th February 1982, 20-21.

35. Phillipson, C. *Capitalism and the Construction of Old Age*. Macmillan, London, 1982.

36. Oliver, M. 'The Politics of Disability' *Critical Social Policy*. 11, 1984, 21-32.

37. Wolfensberger, W. *Normalisation*. Leonard Crainford, 1972.

38. Thomas, D. et al. *Encor – a Way Ahead.* Campaign for the Mentally Handicapped, London, 1978.

39. Dalley, G. 'Ideologies of Care: a feminist contribution to the debate' *Critical Social Policy*. 8, 1983, 72-81.

40. Heginbotham, C. 'Mental Health Service Developments: a critique of current policies'. In Heginbotham, C. & Richards, H. (Eds.) *Policy, Politics and Mental Health*. Gower, London, forthcoming.

New Problems, New Responses: An Overview

Chris Heginbotham

Mental health services in Britain are little better now than 30 years ago. It has been argued by some that the advent of the neuroleptic drugs (the correct name for the powerful phenothiazine anti-psychotic drugs) which lead to significant reductions in long stay hospital populations, and that reduction in itself, must have created improvements; and to some degree this is true. Yet what has developed is an over-dependence on drugs and as a consequence a continuation of the dominance of the medical model of care. As the hospitals have reduced in size the per capita sum spent for each inpatient has increased even taking account of public expenditure cuts finding their way through to long stay hospital budgets.

Any discussion of the future of mental health services must address the need to find alternatives to the large institutions. Yet no British government since the war has produced a coherent policy for alternatives to institutional care. Some small incremental steps have occurred but it is probably still true that 'community care' in its various forms does not so much have 'all Party support' as 'no Party opposition'. Being against the under-funded institutions and in favour of properly organised alternatives is like being against sin and in favour of honesty, truth and beauty. But that doesn't mean that leading a blame-worthy life is easy or even very exciting! It is not surprising that the detractors of community care, on both sides of the political divide, are only now emerging, as the predictable effects of under-funded community services mean patients dumped in the community just as they were dumped in the institutions, 30 or more years ago.

'Community care' is in Judith Oliver's words 'a slogan without a programme'. The term community care has now become so debased as to be useless. Its opposers use the term pejoratively and its supporters are embarrassed at the simplistic notions the term conjures up which relate little to what they would like to see. It is, however, probably worth exploring the term further. Although neither this essay nor the book are about community care *per se*, it is the all pervading mythology of the term which disinforms much of the debate. Responding to mental illness is about individual and professional approaches to individual mentally ill people, but the structure of mental health services is a major determinant of how that response is made. By clearing up a few misunderstandings about community care we may be able to see more clearly the real problems and some potential solutions.

Community care was the term given to attempts to provide a humanitarian alternative to the huge impersonal long stay institutions. Goffman's analysis [1] of institutional structures and Russell Barton's book [2] on institutional neurosis were two of many important studies which indicated how the huge institutions could never be a therapeutic environment for more than a very short period. The discovery of the phenothiazine anti-psychotic drugs in the early 1950s was clearly of great importance even if only now are some of the serious irredeemable side effects of those drugs being recognised.

Just as important were post war attitudes to unlocking doors and the liberalising approaches to care which led directly to the Mental Health Acts of 1959 (England and Wales) and 1960 (Scotland). This removed overly legalistic controls and improved civil detention procedures. At the same time, as Russell Davies has argued, full employment in the 1950s enabled many patients to leave hospital and find some form of (usually low paid) work. Changing attitudes to deviancy and moral rectitude led to a swift reduction in the detention of those such as unmarried mothers whom society had deemed to be 'morally defective'.

As the 1950s advanced into the 1960s, a growing awareness on the part of politicians and professionals alike fuelled schemes to help patients lead more fulfilled lives. Group homes were started, sheltered workshops sprang up and gradually diverse and unco-ordinated services appeared locally, often through voluntary effort. Following the re-organisation of social service departments in 1970 a number of more enlightened local authorities set about providing alternatives to the large institutions − day centres and some residential care, drop-in and counselling services and more sheltered work − while the voluntary sector in conjunction with housing associations provided more (but still far too little) housing, especially after the Housing Act 1974 opened up further possibilities for housing association funding. Much of this provision was primary social care or after-care, and too little planning or development has taken place of secondary or treatment services in the community.

Unfortunately hardly any of this development was underpinned by any consistent philosophy. The hospitals were rightly seen as under-funded warehouses with a single predominant attitude to care rooted firmly in a medical (and custodial) approach. Although a vision of a new service had been suggested, by Maxwell Jones, Russell Barton, Laing and many others – even by Enoch Powell in his famous 'water towers' speech – the vision somehow was never made explicit nor did it ever gain widespread agreement.

'Community Care' is thus the short title for what its supporters would call a comprehensive local mental health service. The trend to talking of care *by* the community rather than *in* the community has been rejected by those striving for such a comprehensive service. Such an approach is not, or need not be, anti-psychiatry. One of the legacies of the critical and negative reaction to Laing, Esterson and Cooper in the 1960s is that any suggested alternatives to institutions are seen as anti-psychiatry and hence anti-therapeutic. The psychiatric lobby seems so frightened of its two bogeys – its loss of power and its genuine concern for future financing of care – that it reacts adversely even to positive proposals for alternatives. Any comprehensive service will have to put psychiatry, as a medical-scientific discipline, in its rightful place in one corner of the huge plane that we call human emotional or mental distress.

To be meaningful a comprehensive local mental health service is about a concept of citizenship and of rebuilding that citizenship following illness. Any mental health care system must set itself the primary objective, not of cure alone, but of helping the individual to regain his or her place as an autonomous member of society able to live as fulfilled a life as possible within the broad bounds set by whatever continued disability results from illness. Such an approach demands that the service starts with the needs of the individual and provides as flexible an approach to care appropriate to the individual's unique needs. This is not an individualistic philosophy though. For example, it is not about propping the patient up and, once on his own two feet, expecting him to care for himself; nor is it about dumping patients back on to informal carers with no support and little income. A properly developed community care service would support and enhance but not cut across appropriate informal caring networks, yet would provide professional help and mandatory income to those informal carers who do wish to provide support to their relatives. As Beresford and Croft [3], Groves and Finch [4], and Finch [5] have pointed out, a major gap in the debate about community care is that related to gender and the role of the euphemistically labelled 'informal carers'.

It would appear that the British government's current attitude is to see cuts in health expenditure throwing more care on to women. The argument runs as follows: unemployment has put women out of work, and closing institutions without alternatives throws the patients on to their women relatives. Eighty per cent of carers are women; and anyway 70 per cent of disabled people are even now looked after in the community by such carers. A 'real' localised mental health care service would provide income, pensions, holidays and respite care for carers as well as supportive professional help.

Finally any developed community alternatives must include participation by the consumer of those services, by carers, and by local communities. Such an approach is difficult to set up and needs a lot of thought, practical concern and power sharing. As a more individual approach has been taken there has been a trend to use the term 'consumer' instead of patient. But is the patient truly a consumer? If a patient has the right to be involved in all decisions about treatment or care, is civil detention *ever* appropriate and, if it is, when is paternalism justified. And further, if the consumer is paramount, at what point does the consumer become the employer, and who is the consumer then? Finally, do unpaid carers count as consumers?

It will be clear from the foregoing that this chapter is promoting a particular view of what 'care in the community', or local mental health care, means, and that this is very different to the perception of government and what a number of commentators see empirically that care in the community has become. The real present danger is that lack of proper planning and financing will undermine the humanitarian aspects of what good community care should be, and lead to a retrenchment on the hospitals. It must be remembered that the hospitals themselves are just another form of failed approach, and that a new way forward is needed.

There are however a number of myths around the idea of developing a local mental health service. The first is that 'community care' is a cheap option. Clearly if a comprehensive mental health service is developed which can respond flexibly to individual need, then it is not and cannot be a cheap option. While we should all be rightly critical of the government's attitude towards developing community care we should not see that as a reason for abandoning the concept.

A second myth is that community care is about shifting resources and services from the health service on to social services departments of local authorities. Such a simplistic notion has gained considerable credibility, but for both pragmatic and professional reasons this cannot be the way forward. Local authorities are becoming increasingly reluctant or unable to take on the caring function mainly for financial reasons and largely because the government's rate capping and rate support grant penalties have undermined even the ability of sympathetic local authorities to act. It is indeed a sad irony that those local authorities which have most assiduously pursued the government's policy of community care are those which are most heavily in financial penalty or with tight rate cap limits. Pragmatically the way forward will be to develop a community *health* service by shifting money out of the large hospitals to provide a large degree of health funded and health managed care. Yet this must be in communities served and wherever possible under collaborative management with social services departments, authorities, housing agencies and the voluntary and private sector.

The third myth about community care is that the country cannot afford it. Although our mental health services have been grossly under-funded for far too long and there is evidently a need for substantial injections of more money, there is nonetheless around 1 billion per annum spent on the large mental hospitals at an average per capita cost (1983-84) of £12,090. The cost of hospitals is little different to the average cost of providing decent community facilities. Almost 45 per cent of hospital costs go on the so called 'hotel' charges – laundry, catering, cleaning, building maintenance and administration. Those functions are needed in the hospitals as currently constituted but a more localised service could use the money and the staff in better and more effective ways. This would of course require staff re-training and re-deployment to a more directly caring function – and needs staff involvement in the planning process. The huge backlog maintenance costs which have built up in the large hospitals are another potential source of development finance for community services.

Fourth, local care is not only about primary care. A comprehensive local service will include secondary care, treatment services and asylum. Making local secondary care a reality is a major challenge – the temptation to spend all the money on the 'worried well' (in Douglas Bennett's phrase) must be avoided.

Lastly, community care is not about one form of funding mechanism. Too many commentators have latched on to one government circular issued in 1983 [6] which expanded the use of joint funding of services and provided for a pilot projects programme, as if this was THE mechanism for care in the community. In Scotland this is known as 'support finance'. Such a view is naive and simplistic, but derives from the lack of any other government response or leadership to developing local alternatives in place of the large hospitals.

So far this chapter has been somewhat abstract and has not considered the differing responses needed to deal with mental illness. Yet we cannot consider the detail of those responses without considering both the nature of mental illness itself, the difficulties with the current responses and the problems associated with developing better alternative methods of care. This is not the place to go into detailed descriptions of mental illness. But it is important to see mental illness as a wide range of responses to personal distress with causations which could be rooted biologically but are more likely determined by individual psychopathology or social and environmental stress of one sort or another. The technical response must thus be flexible and able to respond to a wide range of 'illness' with a wide range of treatment and care options; wherever possible these must relate directly to the individual's life and be provided, as suggested above, in the least restrictive environment and the most valued setting appropriate to the needs of that individual.

Even putting aside the substantial arguments which could be generated by the preceding paragraph, there are still many other problems. In the first place we lack agreement between professionals and politicians, between health services and communities, and between professional groups. We lack an agreed philosophy of care and sometimes any dialogue at all. We lack a political consensus and the political will to develop real alternatives to the large institutions. We lack sufficient cash or flexible funding mechanisms to make care in the community a real alternative. We lack planning mechanisms geared to the vision of the new service we want to create and have only those bureaucratic mechanisms developed for an overly centralised health care management. We lack good models of care to demonstrate to staff the alternatives to hospitals and we lack the managerial will to put these alternatives into practice. These difficulties are exacerbated by some members of the medical profession in the large hospitals who block the development of local care. In addition the rather precious professionalism of some local authority social services staff, rooted, perhaps in a left centred radical social work model of the 1970s, has failed to consider the sorts of flexible alternatives now required. At the same time when the government clearly sees care in the community as a cheap option and a way of dumping patients back on to informal carers, there must be some sympathy for those who wish to see an alternative caring network set up. As Derricourt [7] has said:

'The lack of government response to its own policy initiative in 'Care in the Community' is clearly part and parcel of a monetarist approach to social welfare in which the strategies of promoting voluntary community care, reduction of social services expenditure, restructuring social service departments and the privatisation of potentially profitable sections of the welfare state are combined, and justified by the doctrine of the 'finite cake'. This doctrine seeks to present as uncontentious both cuts in the housing programme between

1980/81 and the end of 1982/83 and the real increases in defence spending.'

So our problems are manifest and not aided by the continuing disagreement about genericism or specialism in social work, the lack of any sort of clear guidance coming out of recent reports such as the Barclay Report, and now the requirements of the Mental Health Act 1983 (England and Wales) or 1984 (Scotland).

The changes which the 1983 Acts have heralded can be stated fairly simply in broad outline. They are: improvements in the civil detention process with a tightening up of ways in which detention is undertaken in the first place, and a speedier resort to mental health review tribunals following detention; the introduction of consent or/and a second opinion for a number of classes of treatment; the provision of the six hour holding power for nurses; the requirement to train and employ approved social workers who will be required to ascertain that the detention of an individual is undertaken in the least restrictive environment appropriate to the needs of that client; the removal of mentally handicapped people by and large from the remit of the act; the provision of guardianship orders; and the creation of the Mental Health Act Commission which has powers to visit all hospitals where there are detained patients, to provide reports on patients and on hospital procedures, to approve doctors for the purposes of giving second opinions, and to produce a code of guidance on the operation of the Act, particularly the consent provisions.

The new Act(s) certainly have thrown up a number of additional problems of detail indicating more serious flaws in our system which must now urgently be addressed. For example it is quite obvious that many nurses, doctors, and other professional staff have very little understanding of the philosophy and jurisprudence underlying the Mental Health Act itself. Few professional staff really understand their duty of care, or their common law rights and responsibilities. As an example many nursing staff approach MIND worried about what they can or cannot do at the end of the six hour holding period which they are now allowed under the 1983 Act. In fact the position at the end of that six hour holding period is really no different to the position they were in previously when they did not have that power and when no responsible medical officer was present. Their common law duties of care and their need to be able to justify any detention has not changed. Social workers are of course also concerned about the role and training of Approved Social Workers and this is now exacerbated by the 'collusion of failure' between the DHSS, the local authority employers and the trade union, NALGO.

The Scottish situation is slightly different. Scotland has had a Mental Welfare Commission since 1960 though three reports in 21 years have not suggested a very toothy watchdog. With only 15 members it is doubtful if it can fulfil its functions adequately; the Mental Health Act Commission, on the other hand, has 90 members drawn from a wide spread of professional and lay people.

Scotland has around 80 per cent more occupied inpatient beds per 1,000 population in comparison to England, which is somewhat strange as local authority powers are rather broader in Scotland. One of the major differences however is on compulsory detention. Scotland does not have a 28 day assessment order. Section 30, the six month order must be reviewed after 28 days by the responsible medical officer. Safeguards on improper detention are less strong with no equivalent to Mental Health Review Tribunals though the patient has the right to a Sheriff Court hearing under certain circumstances. There is no automatic referral thus requiring a seriously ill patient to refer him/herself, perhaps not the most satisfactory approach.

Such important changes have thrown up a host of additional issues to add to those concerned with developing improved local care. Apart from those mentioned above there have been some difficulties in obtaining second opinions for consent and the medical profession especially has been upset by what it sees as a questioning of clinical responsibility. The time scales for mental health review tribunals have caused and are continuing to cause administrative headaches, additional paperwork often leading to delays beyond the statutory time limits for tribunals to be held; and with this the problem of obtaining social work reports. Many social workers in special hospitals and elsewhere too, have refused to obtain home circumstances reports on patients that they did not know or with whom they had had little contact. Patients' rights to a full and fair hearing at the tribunal are undermined, leading to further detention of patients when unnecessary. Discharge following mental health tribunals is made precarious, slowed or even halted due to the unenforceability of the after-care sections of the Act. Although Section 117 allows for health authorities and social service departments to make provision for patients who were detained, the Act does not specify levels of care nor is it written in such a way that there is an individual entitlement. Many patients are still residing in the large overcrowded institutions when they could have left if social service and health authorities had collaboratively provided appropriate residential care or support locally.

RESPONSES

All of these 'problems' require new responses. Although some danger of idealism arises in considering alternative caring mechanisms, a vision must be developed of the caring service that is needed. That vision should be kept in focus constantly while services are developed incrementally. One response, usually from those on the political left, is to become so brow beaten by the government's current lack of care and concern, exemplified by the lack of money, as to suggest that nothing should be done until more money is made available. Constantly harping on the government's failure is a smoke screen to the serious obstacles put up by some psychiatrists (and to some extent the social work profession) and fails to recognise that by unlocking the 1 billion spent every year in the large hospitals much could be provided as an alternative. With this must go a new planning mechanism geared to the vision rather than to old fashioned bureaucratic and centrist approaches to health service development. There must be a mechanism for participation of local communities and the development of local forums for ascertaining need on a plural basis rather than solely on the needs of those currently in the large hospitals – which is all that is done by too many health authorities at present. At the same time new approaches must be evaluated. Clear objectives for human service delivery should be set.

Crisis intervention will be a major part of a total flexible approach. Crisis intervention is both a necessary component of mental health care for discharged patients, as well as contributing to a preventive approach. Elsewhere in this book crisis intervention is considered in some detail. The authors conclude that the new Act has not succeeded 'by itself' in 'safeguarding the rights of mentally ill people' as the proportion of emergency admissions is still higher than if used only for exceptional cases. Lack of co-ordination and constraints on service development seem more detrimental to crisis service than any problem of inter-professional relationships. Figures from one hospital – the Royal Southampton – show that between 1981/82 and 1983/84 the total number of compulsory admissions declined from 166 to 129 – but are now creeping up slightly. The bulk of admissions are under Part II and of those, the use of S3 and S4 have halved whereas those under S4 (the three day emergency order) have almost doubled.

Reasons for the overall decline are not clear. It may have something to do with a 'greater consistency in not admitting compulsorily those willing patients who are thought likely to change their minds' [8] – stemming ironically from the extension of compulsory powers through the nurses' six hour section (S5.4). Section 2 is being used as a short term treatment order rather than an assessment order. This is curious as patients under S3 do not *have* to stay any longer than those under S2 (the 28 day order), and S3 patients do obtain the benefit of entitlement to after-care under S117.

One rather worrying trend is the use of S3 for patients on almost permanent leave from hospital. The legality of this practice is in some dispute, though there is a need to consider some form of community treatment order. The matter turns on whether a person has the right to risk relapse with the background protection of a full admission procedure rather than be kept on a compulsory order indefinitely. Such an approach might also become extended to other than the small group of highly vulnerable patients.

Police powers under the Act are subject to some scrutiny. The use of S136 must be monitored more closely, as must the role of police and the medical profession in dealing with mentally ill offenders. Chiswick, McIsaac and McLintock [9] found

> 'a tension between the police and medical practitioners because the police see medical specialists 'choose' their cases and leave the difficult and violent offenders, as well as the petty or persistent offenders who appear mentally unstable, to the ordinary process of law enforcement and criminal justice.'

The other major issue related to the Mental Health Act is consent (or dissent). As Bingley puts it:

> 'The 1983 Act has done a curious double-hander: it has overturned the assumption that an individual's legal status (ie if detained) was sufficient to dispense with an examination of an individual's ability to comprehend the nature, purpose and likely effect of treatment; at the same time it has written down that patients can in certain circumstances have treatment imposed on them. The net result.... is that the second opinion procedures have [had] no effect on practice as far as discernible' [10].

The second opinion process appears to be having more of a 'placebo' effect than demonstrating that patients' wishes are really being taken into account.

If we are to move towards the development of a new approach there will have to be collaborative management of some services locally between health, housing, social services and the voluntary sector. The development of a localised comprehensive mental health service, rather than using some glib buzz word such as 'community care' demands a sharing of resources, of ideology and an involvement of consumers, carers and local communities. The social work role in this is complex requiring a flexible response between localised care with specialist back up. The continuing attempt by social work staff to 'have it both ways' must cease. Change is inevitable yet does not mean wholeheartedly going for one system as opposed to another. Many lament the passing of psychiatric social workers and the move from social workers having 'superior psychological insight' to having 'superior sociological insight' [11]. It is a lamentable fact that too many professional social workers see themselves as above guidance or supervision yet are increasingly vociferous in their opposition to taking personal responsibility for clients. Many seem unhappy that the Mental Health Act continues to place personal responsibility for the civil detention of clients on social workers rather than vesting that responsibility in the local authority. Such a position can only lead to a diminution of the social work ethic and eventually to the demise of social work as practised over the last 20 years. As Ruth Wilkes has stated:

> 'Far from neglecting the social factor the modern social worker sees society as being all important;... it is no longer the individual who is at fault but the social and economic system and the social worker has been born to put it right. The approach is puritanical, joyless and frighteningly dedicated. The presenting problem is still not the real problem' [12].

If social work is to regain its credibility with clients and the general public alike it will have to re-develop a professionalism based on a code of ethics concerned with the individual and not some broader sociology. At the same time social work and other professions must become accountable to the clients and the communities they serve. That accountability can derive from the ballot box and hence from elected members, but it can also come from offering the client a service by fully trained, appropriately deployed professionals who understand their task and are there to do their very best for that individual according to that individual's needs as expressed from time to time.

Of course all of this begs the question of what are the client's real needs as opposed to the client's possible wants and how those needs can be assimilated so as to enable a supportive service to be planned, yet which can then respond flexibly to those who require that service.

What is probably required is for social work, psychiatry, psychology and other paramedical staff to re-think the ethic on which they base their service approach. The radical social work model of the 1970s has had little effect on the political system, and it could be argued has been contributory to the neolibertarian spirit which informs the present government's dogma. A reaction to left wing welfarist notions has certainly aided those forces destructive of the welfare state. An approach based on generally held values may be more appropriate. In a multi-cultural and multi-racial society these values must reflect the sort of communities which make up that society; but an approach which is based on the values to which most people would subscribe will lead to a more individually centred approach, rather than one based on some remote professional approach rooted in social and political action as opposed to the direct and obvious needs of the individual client.

Finally, within these responses, we urgently need a re-appraisal of the funding of mental health care both to accelerate and enhance cash injections into the development of alternatives to hospitals, and in providing central funding for equivalent types of care based on the needs of clients. At present there is considerable 'ad hocery' around the funding of even similar types of care whether provided by the private sector, voluntary agencies, or local authorities and the health service. Manpower watch figures which now apply to the health service as well as local authorities, undermine the efforts of health administrators to develop alternative staff intensive patterns of care within existing budgets; and current government financial policies towards local government create severe disincentives to any form of transfer mechanisms from health to local government, and undermine collaborative approaches to the development of community services.

CONCLUSION

Mental health services are in a mess. We have a service polarised between a centralised bureaucratic health service based on large institutional hospitals, and a fragmented community service made up of social service departments, housing departments, the voluntary sector and private sector provision. We do not have a shared vision of the sort of service we would like to see; we have patients dumped in a community that does not care and has not the resources to care, yet we cannot allow retrenchment on the large hospitals which themselves are only another form of dump. We urgently require dialogue between all professionals involved to consider honestly and openly the description of a properly supported caring and treatment service available as locally as possible, in the least restrictive environment and so it is available to meet need flexibly wherever it arises. It may take a long time before we could get to that service description. But it surely is a truism that if we had the chance again we would not start from here! We would not re-build 70, 1,000-bed mental hospitals.

In summary many of the requirements set out above mirror the four points developed by Hadley and Hatch [13]. They argued that an alternative approach needed four main features:

plural provision;

decentralisation implying flatter structures, a different interpretation of professionalism and re-inforcement of support to informal carers;

contractual accountability;

participation of consumers, carers and community.

To these could be added:

a shared vision of care based on valued options able to respond to individual need and aimed at enhancing citizenship;

local collaborative approaches;

recognition of the realities of life in financing of the service;

a planning system geared to the vision of the future, diversified service.

Pluralism does not necessarily mean deregulation or a cheap option, but can mean greater cost benefit and value as long as this does not lead to exploitation of carers, workers or clients. Too much energy is presently spent, to the detriment of clients, on a polarised debate between a neo-libertarian right bent on privatisation at all costs, and a collectivist left concerned to oppose all alternatives to state finance *and* production. Britain has always had pluralism. Voluntary and private sector innovation has often been the catalyst to improved care. Defending state bureaucracies, professional demarcations and control over resources will not help the client; nor will hand wringing while government pursues private provision at any cost. We need a new way forward.

References

1. Goffman, E. *Stigma – Notes on the Management of Spoiled Identity*. Pelican, London, 19.

2. Barton, W. Russell *Institutional Neurosis*. John Wright & Sons, Bristol, 1959.

3. Beresford, P. & Croft, S. 'Welfare Pluralism: the new face of Fabianism' *Critical Social Policy*. 9, Spring 1984, Sheffield CSP Ltd.

4. Finch, J. & Groves, D. *A Labour of Love*. Routledge & Kegan Paul, London, 1983.

5. Finch, J. 'Community Care: developing non-sexist alternatives' *Critical Social Policy*. 9, Spring 1984, Sheffield CSP Ltd.

6. *Health Service Development – Care in the Community and Joint Finance*. DHSS HC(83)6/LAC(83)5, London, 1983.

7. Derricourt, N.J. 'Strategies of Community Care'. In Lovey, M., Boswell, D. & Clarke, J. (Eds.) *Social Policy and Social Welfare*. Open University Press, Milton Keynes, 1983.

8. Bingley, W. in a paper presented to a MIND Conference, May 1985.

9. Chiswick, D., McIsaac, M.W. & McLintock, F.H. *Prosecution of the Mentally Disturbed*. Aberdeen University Press, 1984.

10. Bingley, W. op. cit.

11. Wilkes, R. *Social Work with Underprivileged Groups*. Tavistock, London, 1981.

12. Wilkes, R. op. cit.

13. Hadley, R. & Hatch, S. *Social Welfare and the Failure of the State: Centralised social services and participatory alternatives*. George Allen and Unwin, London, 1981.

DEPARTMENT OF APPLIED SOCIAL STUDIES AND SOCIAL RESEARCH
BARNETT HOUSE
WELLINGTON SQUARE
OXFORD OX1 2ER

SOCIAL SCIENCE LIBRARY

Manor Road Building
Manor Road
Oxford OX1 3UQ
Tel: (2)71093 (enquiries and renewals)
http://www.ssl.ox.ac.uk

This is a NORMAL LOAN item.

We will email you a reminder before this item is due.

Please see http://www.ssl.ox.ac.uk/lending.html
for details on:

- loan policies; these are also displayed on the
  notice boards and in our library guide.

- how to check when your books are due back.

- how to renew your books, including information
  on the maximum number of renewals.
  Items may be renewed if not reserved by
  another reader. Items must be renewed before
  the library closes on the due date.

- level of fines; fines are charged on overdue books.

Please note that this item may be recalled during Term.

303834251T